MEMORIES

The Common Core of European Private Law Series



**Common Core of European Private Law**

1. *Interpretation of Commercial Contracts in European Private Law*, C.J.W. Baaij, D. Cabrelli and L. Macgregor (eds.)
2. *Immoral Contracts in Europe*, A. Colombi Ciacchi, C. Mak, Z. Mansoor (eds.)
3. *The Acquisition of Immovables through Long-Term Use*, B. Hoops and E.J. Marais (eds.)

# MEMORIES

Rudolf B. Schlesinger

*Edited by*
Ugo Mattei
Andrea Pradi

INTERSENTIA

Cambridge – Antwerp – Chicago

Intersentia Ltd
8 Wellington Mews
Wellington Street | Cambridge
CB1 1HW | United Kingdom
Tel: +44 1223 736 170
Email: mail@intersentia.co.uk
www.intersentia.com | www.intersentia.co.uk

*Distribution for the UK and*
*Rest of the World (incl. Eastern Europe)*
NBN International
1 Deltic Avenue, Rooksley
Milton Keynes MK13 8LD
United Kingdom
Tel: +44 1752 202 301 | Fax: +44 1752 202 331
Email: orders@nbninternational.com

*Distribution for Europe*
Lefebvre Sarrut Belgium NV
Hoogstraat 139/6
1000 Brussels
Belgium
Tel: +32 (0)800 39 067
Email: mail@intersentia.be

*Distribution for the USA and Canada*
Independent Publishers Group
Order Department
814 North Franklin Street
Chicago, IL 60610
USA
Tel: +1 800 888 4741 (toll free) | Fax: +1 312 337 5985
Email: orders@ipgbook.com

Memories

Artwork on cover: Dan Totilca / Alamy Stock Photo

ISBN 978-1-83970-276-1
D/2022/7849/84
NUR 822

British Library Cataloguing in Publication Data. A catalogue record for this book is available from the British Library.

*Dear Children and Grandchildren,*

*Each of us is an individual, distinct and different from everyone else. One's individuality, however, does not come about in a wholly fortuitous way. One's personality is formed by myriad impulses, some of which may be traceable to genes inherited from ancestors or to impressions and experiences accumulated over a lifetime. Among those impressions and experiences, those gathered from one's elders in the course of a shared family life are apt to be particularly strong and formative.*

*Thus – through shared and inherited family traditions as well as through genes – each of us carries in his body and mind a complex legacy of traits and attitudes that stem from our families past. For this reason, it may be an aid to self-knowledge to learn as much as possible about the lives, the views and the personalities of one's parents and more distant ascendants.*

*To assist you in this learning process, I am herewith recording some facts concerning my own life and the lives of my parents and grandparents facts with which many of you are unfamiliar and which would be lost to you and to future generations if they were not written down while I am able to do so.*

*I shall put down the facts as they leap out of my memory, without paying too much attention to systematicity and organization. In general, however, I shall try to proceed chronologically, reporting what I have been told about my ancestors before I talk about my own life.*

# FOREWORD

## A Lucky Man: On a New Edition of Professor Schlesinger's Memoir

It is a unique honor to present to the international community a new edition of Professor Rudolf Schlesinger's memoir. The first edition was published in 2000, not long after his death, at the University of Trento, the first home of the Common Core of European Private Law project, which launched there in 1993. This second edition was made possible by the generous funding of Justitierådet Edvard Cassels Stiftelse and the organization by Stockholm University of the 27th General Meeting, on March 3 and 4, 2022, of the Common Core project, the oldest ongoing collective study on European private law.[1]

At the meeting in Stockholm, a plenary session was dedicated to commemorating Professor Schlesinger on the 25th anniversary of his death in San Francisco on November 10, 1996.[2] I was invited, as his successor at the University of California Hastings College of the Law, to deliver the commemoration speech (mostly reproduced in this foreword).

We learn from his memoir, conceived and beautifully written as a legacy to his family, that Professor Schlesinger – Rudi for family and friends – graduated *summa cum laude* in Munich in 1933, the very year of the rise of Hitler to the Chancellorship. As a Jew, Rudi had to rush to defend his dissertation and he was able to do so shortly before the Nazi regime would ban Jewish students from graduating. In Germany, legal positivism, in the form of Nazi law, began to show its grimmest face. The global prestige of German law, with its claim of scientific perfection that was able to influence Langdell during the establishment of Harvard Law

---

1 *See* Mauro Bussani and Ugo Mattei, *The Common Core Approach to the European Private Law*, 3 Colum. J. Eur. L. 339 (1997). For updates on the output of the project with some 20 volumes published and many others in the pipeline, *see* www.commoncore.org.

2 *See* Richard Buxbaum and Ugo Mattei, *Rudolph B. Schlesinger 1909–1996*, 45 Am. J. Comp. L. 1 (1997).

School in 1870 and to maintain global leadership in legal scholarship through the anti-formalistic development initiated by Rudolf Von Jhering, was beginning its sudden and tragic decline.[3]

Rudi left Europe in 1938, and soon after started Columbia Law School which, together with Yale, was then the most important center of legal realism, ultimately a progressive adaptation of Jhering's. Thus, when Rudi joined Cornell in 1948, he had experienced and internalized the best of the two dominant Western legal systems at the passage of the global torch of legal hegemony from Germany to the US. He attended law school in Munich at the top of German prestigiousness, before the collapse that followed the yielding of dominant legal culture to Nazism. The justification of the so-called "dual State" – based, on the one hand, on the unpredictable irrationality of the *Führerprinzip* and, on the other hand, on the predictable rationality of the legal framework of market transactions – was ultimately a legal project. He attended Columbia when legal realism was offering the best academic legal minds to the making and preservation of the New Deal institutions,[4] before the Cold War and McCarthyism would stifle progressive political developments, paving the way for de-politicization in the form of the legal process movement (and later law and economics).

Rudi was a lucky man, as he acknowledges in this memoir on which he continued to work until the very end, when fortune turned its back on him in the form of Putti's disease, when he was still a youthful, incredibly bright scholar.

Compared with other towering figures who immigrated from Germany (as a paradoxical gift of the Führer to the free world: jurists like Rabel, Ehrenzweig, Kirchheimer, and many others[5]), he arrived younger in the US and was the only one who went through a full process of legal education in both legal traditions, rendering him the only truly bijural scholar in America. The teaching of law within a comparative framework was thus natural to him. His formation determined the true birth of comparative law as a full-fledged autonomous academic discipline in the US.

---

3 *See* Ugo Mattei, *Why the Wind Changed. Intellectual Leadership in Western Law*, 42 Am. J. Comp. L. 195 (1994). *See also generally* The Reception of Continental Ideas in the Common Law World 1820–1920 (Mathias Reimann ed., 1993).

4 *See* Morton J. Horwitz, The Transformation of American Law, 1870–1960: The Crisis of Orthodoxy, at 169 ff. (1992).

5 *See* Der Einfluss deutscher Emigranten auf die Rechtsentwicklung in den USA und in Deutschland (Marcus Lutter, Ernst C. Stiefel, and Michael H. Hoeflich eds., 1993); Ernst C. Stiefel and Frank Mecklenburg, Deutsche Juristen im amerikanischen Exil (1933–1950) (1991).

In fact, this memoir is not the first book of Rudi's that was *not*, because of his proverbial and ironic modesty, intended to be published. Schlesinger's COMPARATIVE LAW, the legendary casebook (that reached its seventh edition in 2009) that, together with René David's in France, and Zweigert and Kötz's in Germany, has generated modern comparative law, was similarly meant to be a private set of materials in the relationship between Rudi and his Cornell students. I can witness, because I took his class at Hastings in the spring of 1988, how devoting his time and best energy to students was Rudi's genuine vocation, in an era in which there was no marketing strategy by law schools (as today) to entice students into a very expensive investment by emphasizing the faculty commitment to excellence in teaching.

Rudi founded comparative law in the genuinely realist paradigm of functionalism and social science that fascinated him at Columbia, enriched by his quasi-mathematical passion for precision and relevant details that make the great formalist continental jurist. The mix was a big bang for the discipline and, through the experience of the Cornell project in the 1960s, would pave the way for the functionalist-structuralism of later developments, especially in Italy through the work of Rodolfo Sacco in private law.[6] Procedure was to Rudi the real laboratory for comparative law, and I remember, with a degree of nostalgia and of relief (not to have to deal with it anymore) the long hours spent on the difference between claim preclusion, issue preclusion, and continental *res judicata*!

The era of Cold-War technocracy naturally attracted US realists, and Rudi was no exception, even if his desire of understanding radically limited his participation in the ideological construction of the free world.[7] The confrontation with Soviet Russia was always there, and we witness in the tragic events of today that its ideology never disappeared. Schlesinger was grateful to America, to the "free world" that allowed him to escape the Nazis. However, his gratitude (that exudes from this memoir) never made him part of the ideological apparatuses of the US self-aggrandizing rhetoric of human rights and the rule of law. He expressed his gratitude through the constant exercise of severe critique. "Only if you criticize what you love can you improve it". This is a teaching that I never forgot,

---

6 *See* Ugo Mattei, *The Comparative Jurisprudence of Schlesinger and Sacco. A Study in Legal Influence*, in RETHINKING THE MASTERS OF COMPARATIVE LAW 237–256 (Annelise Riles ed., 2001).

7 *See* Ugo Mattei, *The Cold War and Comparative Law: A Reflection on the Politics of Intellectual Discipline*, 65 AM. J. COMP. L. 567 (2017).

and that should always be kept in mind by those that believe in freedom and in the potential of law in making a just society. Unfortunately, today, even on academic campuses, critique is confused with lack of loyalty or of patriotism.

I met Rudi at a peculiar time in my life. Two years before the fall of the Berlin Wall, it was a relatively optimistic time, not only personally (I was becoming a father, and now I am becoming a grandfather!) but also academically and politically. The end of history,[8] with its unbearable self-congratulatory rhetoric, was not in sight. I remember my first visit to Moscow in 1985, when the equilibrium of the Cold War still seemed eternal, and I remember many discussions with Rudi on the comparative merits of the market and the plan. Yet, many of the movements that under full-fledged neoliberalism took their reactionary gloves off (like law and economics) were still scholarly paradigms that many of us in Europe thought could actually help go beyond the excesses of black letter formalism and bureaucracy affecting the civil law tradition. On my side, it was love at first sight. Rudi was a marvel, and this memoir written for his children and grandchildren makes it evident without any filter. Humble, witty, self-ironic, warm, thoughtful, caring, incredibly knowledgeable, optimistic … I may be biased by personal gratitude and nostalgia, but I cannot find one defect!

One day in early 1993 I received a letter from Professor Schlesinger (a real one, like those of the past century) in my mailbox at the University of Trento telling me that his eyesight was fading and that he needed someone to replace him in teaching comparative law at Hastings and asking whether I was available. Of course, I said, and shortly after that my second life in the San Francisco Bay Area started. Hastings was then run by leading civil procedure scholar Mary Kay Kane, who was a student of Rudi's at Cornell and probably considered herself bound by Rudi's choices in comparative law by *stare decisis*.

My father passed away in September 1993, and that was the moment Professor Schlesinger became Rudi to me. He was only five years older than my father, and he naturally filled the void. A little more than three years later, I realized how hard Rudi's departure was for me.

The post-Cold War change to the balance of global power, especially the humiliation of Russia (whose consequences, similarly to those of Versailles, we are now experiencing), radicalized by politics, and my

8 *See* Francis Fukuyama, The End of History and the Last Man (1992).

first book in English, COMPARATIVE LAW AND ECONOMICS (University of Michigan Press 1997), began to question the political neutrality and desirability of law and economics. Rudi was hugely influential in getting the book published. He wrote one of the evaluation letters, as well as a blurb.

The day before his and Putti's final and dramatic act of freedom, he invited me over to San Francisco, telling me over the phone he had something to discuss with me. I was in Berkeley; I thought it was about the manuscript. I was too lazy to cross the Bay Bridge, and I declined his invitation and said I would see him the day after. The next time I saw him was at his funeral: I will always regret that missed opportunity of a last goodbye.

The Common Core of European Private Law was born as an early product of our acquaintance. The idea, abundantly discussed with Rudi as early as 1992, was to apply and upgrade the methodology of the Cornell Common Core Project on the formation of contracts,[9] tailoring it to the European context. Both method and spirit have evolved, but to me, 27 years after its launch, the role of General Editor has remained a matter of identification with Rudi. From the human perspective, it has been my way to honor a mentor. From the scholarly perspective, it is a unique occasion to compare the law, rather than tediously discussing how we should do it. From the political perspective, I regard it as an attempt to save the Western Legal Tradition, globally dominant after the demise of socialist law, from the pattern of decay created by academic chauvinism and parochialism. I am not sure we succeeded, but we did our best.

There is clearly the trace of Rudi's optimism in trying to enrich functionalism (that was the main tool of US legal technocracy) with the nitty-gritty details of Italian legal structuralism, à la Sacco, another mentor who has just passed away whom I will miss (Sacco introduced three generations of Italian comparatists to the methodology of the factual approach developed at Cornell by Rudi 60 years ago). Certainly, the early work with Mauro Bussani, Jim Gordley, Franz Werro, Mathias Reimann, Antonio Gambaro, and many others in developing a methodological standard capable of merging the approaches of these two towering figures has been one of the intellectual pleasures of my life.

---

9 *See* FORMATION OF CONTRACTS. A STUDY ON THE COMMON CORE OF LEGAL SYSTEMS, 2 Vols. (Rudolf B. Schlesinger ed., 1968). The volumes containing the results of the so-called Cornell Seminars were reviewed by huge figures like Jeffrey Hazard, Max Rheinstein, and Rodolfo Sacco.

Optimism lingered for a while, but it incrementally became clear (at least to me) that the geopolitics of Europe makes it very unlikely that a European model can become the next torch of legal hegemony, capable of succeeding the intellectually-declining US law. European legal scholars, I believe, proved incapable of developing a common identity, no matter how fluid, or of opening the treasure box of legal traditions formerly within the Soviet block of influence. The problems resulting from national legal parochialism (those that have impeded European codification) and from Western European arrogance have been met by a somewhat uncritical semi-peripheral reception of US law. The result is that, today, Europe follows the intellectual decline of the US neoliberal model that it stubbornly (even if only acoustically) follows.[10]

Professor Schlesinger was a lucky man. He was able to enjoy the peak of legal scholarship in the US, contributing much to its global impact. He believed that continental Europe, once a crib of legality, could function, once hybridized with the common law tradition, as a robust guarantee that the horrors he escaped would not return.[11]

Rudi never saw the brutal decline of the rule of law in the US after September 11, 2001. He never saw political partisanship hijacking the US Supreme Court. He could not even imagine the politically correct morphing into cancel culture closing the American mind. He never saw war once again in the heart Europe. He did not have to witness propaganda taking over knowledge and understanding, not only in the media but also in many mainstream scholarly circles. Nor did he have to witness the generalized disrespect of values, such as dignity and even formal equality, in interpreting the logic of emergency to force millions of unwilling citizens in Europe into submitting to forms of electronic control of their sanitary status in violation of the Nuremberg code. What would Rudi have thought in front of these legal horrors visited upon us?

Rudi Schlesinger died without seeing the decline of the very idea of Western law, as a rational and dialectical way to solve conflicts, substituted by the rise of devices of prediction and surveillance based on the logic of algorithms.[12] I cannot imagine a critical and inquisitive mind like

---

10 *See* Ugo Mattei, THE EUROPEAN CODIFICATION PROCESS. CUT & PASTE (2003).

11 *See* Rudolf Schlesinger, *The Past and the Future of Comparative Law*, 43 AM. J. COMP. L. 477 (1995), acceptance speech of the doctorate *honoris causa* received in Trento and his last published piece.

12 *See* Ugo Mattei, *Do Smart Things Make Us Dumb? Reflection on the Addiction Crisis of Cyborg Consumerism*, EUR. J. CONS. L. 613 (2020). *See also* Joshua A.T. Fairfield, OWNED: PROPERTY, PRIVACY, AND THE NEW DIGITAL SERFDOM (2017).

Rudi's accepting the logic of *de facto* conditionality, "take-it-or-leave-it", the blackmail that has domesticated our fundamental sense of justice and freedom of choice over the Internet, where it is absolutely normal that the rules are made by the platforms and that might is right.

In thinking back to Rudi and to his teaching, a quarter of a century since his death, I feel nostalgia for a pattern of legal civilization that is gone and will not return. I also wonder, looking towards the global future, if the torch of legal hegemony is not passing into the hands of cultures that have only paid lip service to the ideology of the rule of law. Systems, such as that of China, are providing to Western law, perhaps already a Western despotism in the making, institutional devices of economic control capable of cheaply substituting law as a controlling process.[13]

This memoir that you are about to enjoy will plunge you into a legal and academic world that seems more different from ours today than "far Eastern" models based on despotic technological control towards which we are converging. With the transformation of control technologies, models that we used to describe as oriental despotism might be the future hegemony in global law.

Spending time with Rudi is like reading a novel capable of distracting from a grim present. Our task as critical intellectuals "on the shoulders of Schlesinger"[14] should be to recreate some of the conditions necessary to share the marvelous optimism that stems from the life of a lucky man.

Ugo Mattei
University of California, Berkeley,
March 23, 2022

---

13 *See* Ugo Mattei, Liu Guanghua and Emanuele Ariano, *The Chinese Advantage in Emergency Law*, 21(1) GLOBAL JURIST 1 (2021).

14 See Vivian Curran, *On the Shoulders of Schlesinger: The Trento Common Core of European Private Law Project*, 2(2) GLOBAL JURIST FRONTIERS https://doi.org/10.2202/1535-1653.1063 (2003).

# EDITOR'S NOTE

Rudolf B. Schlesinger passed away four years ago. His long life has allowed him to witness, almost entirely, the past century.

The comparative law community is gathering in New Orleans to celebrate the past century of comparative legal studies. A century that has been dominated by a handful of great masters. We believe that this international scholarly community regards R.B. Schlesinger as the Master of Masters and the past century as the century of Rudolf B. Schlesinger.

At the Cornell Common Core Project, R.B. Schlesinger has taught to us a methodology that is today more lively than ever. His case-book is still the "big dog" in the field. In his work for the New York Law Revision Commission he has showed to us the potentials of our discipline for law reform.

We believe that the comparative law community – those who had the fortune to know and to love him in person, as well as those younger ones who did not have this chance – would be eager to know more about this exceptional man. And we also believe that the best way to know about a person is to let him talk.

The Memories we have the honor to present fulfill this quest. But since he was a major intellectual leader, they also fulfill a need in understanding and self-consciousness of an entire scholarly community, which faces unprecedented challenges.

In these memories Rudolf B. Schlesinger talks about himself with the usual understated and simple attitude that stems also from his scholarship and that we have learned to love. He talks to his offspring as a grandfather in his armchair, addressing the horrors of Nazi brutality but also the chances and casual contingencies that made him the great master of our field. In doing so, however, he also discusses the historical roots of an intellectual posture that determines much of our current way of thinking about comparative law. Indeed he shows us, once more, the historically contingent nature of such way of thinking. Most importantly for the comparativist, he tells us the relevant story of a century in which the intellectual enterprise that we call comparative law has claimed scientific status.

Unfortunately, the memories have not been completed because of tragic circumstances he once referred to with the phrase: "Fortune turned its back to me". But when he left us he was conscious that the main part of the job was accomplished. He has been able to describe the process of seeding, knowing that the harvest has been so abundant that other people could easily describe it (See note to the reader at the beginning of Chapter 12)

As readers of these memories, we have to be grateful to Rudi for leaving us this last important intellectual legacy. We must be grateful to his family – to Fay and Steve in particular – to have agreed to share with us (and with Rudi's intellectual community) these pages so specially written for them.

As editors, we are particularly grateful to the Law Department of the University of Trento (where Rudolf B. Schlesinger was awarded an Honorary Degree in 1995) and in particular to its director, Professor Diego Quaglioni for making this publication possible. Possibly in no other institution is Schlesinger's memory so alive. Every year, during the days devoted to discussing the results of the search for the Common Core of European Private Law, he is with us. We are also thankful to Dean Mary Kay Kane of the University of California, Hastings College of the Law, where Rudolf Schlesinger taught for his last twenty years, for participating in this publication project. Finally we need to thank the "Associazione R.B. Schlesinger for the study of European Law" for further funding. Gordon van Kessel and Elisabetta Grande have helped in the final preparation of the manuscript and we wish to thank them too.

The book has been published in record time and this would not have been possible without the help of Ted Jang and Michelle Sharoni at Hastings and Carla Boninsegna at Trento.

Ugo Mattei and Andrea Pradi
University of California,
Hastings College of the Law, San Francisco
25 September 2000*

* This Editorial Note is a reproduction of the Editorial Note from the original publication, published in 2000: RUDOLF B. SCHLESINGER: MEMORIES (Ugo Mattei and Andrea Pradi eds., 2000).

# CONTENTS

# CHAPTER I

# MY FATHER AND HIS FAMILY

The Schlesingers, it appears, at one time lived at or near Erfurt, a town in the German province of Thuringia. During the first half of the nineteenth century my great-grandfather is said to have moved to Berlin. His father (my great-great-grandfather, whose name was Meier Schlesinger), with the help of two successive wives, produced more than a dozen children, with the result that my father and grandfather had a large number of distant cousins with whom they did not maintain much contact.

My grandfather Berthold Schlesinger, whose first name was to become my middle name, was born around 1840. As I shall report forthwith, he died at a very young age, at a time when my father was only one and one-half years old. Thus, my father never really knew his father, and this may be the reason why my father's knowledge of the history of the Schlesinger family was quite limited. Hence also the sketchiness of some of the data reported here.

About my grandfather's early life I know virtually nothing. Certain it is, however, that in the early 1860s, when he was approximately twenty-three or twenty-four years old, he met my grandmother, Cecilia Kraemer, who was several years younger than he. She had been born and raised in the small Bavarian town of Ichenhausen, not far from Augsburg. For reasons unknown to me, Ichenhausen was the home of a relatively large Jewish community, as proven by the fact that many Jewish families in the United States and elsewhere trace their ancestry to Ichenhausen.

My grandparents (Berthold and Cecilia) got married – probably in 1863 or 1864 – and soon after their marriage emigrated to the United States, where they settled down in Philadelphia. I have no firm knowledge concerning their reasons for leaving the Old World, but it is not too difficult to venture a guess. Berthold was a Prussian subject, while Cecilia was Bavarian. A war between Prussia, on one side, and Austria and Bavaria, on the other, was foreseeable at the time. As the history books tell us, that war actually broke out in 1866. My grandfather presumably was not too anxious to fight in the Prussian army in a war against Bavaria, the country of his bride. Thus, the threatening war clouds probably furnished at least one of the reasons for their decision to leave Germany.

Some speculation is possible, also, concerning the basis on which they chose the United States as their new home. And thereby hangs an extraordinary tale.

My grandmother Cecilia had two brothers, Bernhard and Raphael Kraemer. When Raphael was about fourteen years old, he was apparently a somewhat mischievous boy. On a Saturday, when the Jews of Ichenhausen were assembled in worship, young Raphael climbed up to the roof of the Synagogue, and when the worshipers left the Temple, he (it must be confessed) urinated upon their heads.

The whole community, including his parents, took an exceedingly grave view of this offense, and the most severe punishment was meted out. The punishment: he received a one-way steerage class steamship ticket to New York, and no further aid or support from his family. Thus thrown upon the shores of the United States, he had to start at the bottom of society, washing dishes and doing other menial chores. But being a youngster of great energy and shrewdness, he quickly worked his way up, moved from New York to Chicago, and by the time he was twenty seven years old had acquired one million dollars a colossal fortune at that time. Like many other recent immigrants, however, he could not find a wife in his new country. Virtually all of the young immigrants were males, and in the more established families the parents of daughters were unwilling to accept a recent immigrant as a son in law. Thus Raphael, following the example of many other immigrants, had to travel back to the old country in search of a wife. Upon his return to Bavaria, he and a girl named Sophie became attracted to each other.

In accordance with the custom of the time, he asked Sophie's father for her hand. The answer was a conditional yes: he could marry Sophie, provided he gave up any idea of returning to the United States, and settled down in Munich, where Sophie's family lived. Raphael had no choice but to agree to the condition. He married Sophie and settled down in Munich, where he lived until he died at a ripe old age.

Now let me come back to the story of Berthold and Cecilia, my own grandparents. Their plan to leave Germany crystalized just a few years after Raphael's return from the United States and subsequent marriage. As Raphael was Cecilia's elder brother, and was generally regarded as clever and experienced, it was only natural for Cecilia and Berthold to turn to Raphael for advice. On the basis of his own successful experience in the United States, Raphael strongly advised his sister and brother-in-law to migrate to North America. They followed his advice, and in the mid-eighteen-sixties crossed the Atlantic. They settled down in Philadelphia, where my grandfather soon opened a men's clothing store. His business apparently was successful, and he became very active in the organization of the Free Masons.

While they lived in Philadelphia, Cecilia and Berthold had four children. The first one was a girl who was born in 1867 and whom they named Francisca. The second was my father, born on September 6, 1869, who was given the Jewish name Moses and the English-German name Morris-Moritz. In late 1870 or early 1871 Berthold and Cecilia had twins. I do not know the names of the twins; both of them died as infants.

Shortly after the birth of the twins in 1871, a severe typhus epidemic broke out in Philadelphia. My grandfather, as a leading Free Mason, apparently insisted on visiting some of his lodge brothers who were struck by the disease. After a short time he himself caught the disease and died from it in 1871. He is buried in Philadelphia, and I have cared for his grave during the last 50 years.

For my grandmother, who at that time was about twenty-six years of age, the tragedy was compounded by the fact that she was far from her family and that shortly after her husband's death, her two youngest children "the twins" also died. To assist her in this desperate situation, her brother Raphael traveled from Munich to Philadelphia. He persuaded her to return to Munich where she would be closer to her family. Accepting his advice, my grandmother Cecilia, with her two remaining children (Francisca and my father), sailed back to Germany in late 1871. Thus, my father crossed the Atlantic for the first time at the age of two in an eastward direction. My grandmother and her two children settled down in Munich. She never married again, and her life was a most unhappy one. In those days it was practically impossible for a woman to enter a business or profession. Thus, until my father was old enough to support her, she depended largely on the somewhat skimpy charity of her brothers. After my father grew up, her financial situation improved, but her health became more and more precarious. In her older years she suffered from Diabetes and Parkinson's Disease. When she died in 1918, I was almost nine years old.

Thus, I remember her well. As a child I visited her often. She was a good looking, white haired lady; but wholly bedridden. She was paralyzed and constantly trembling as a result of Parkinson's Disease. Her mind, however, was completely clear and she often talked about the few years of happiness that had been granted to her, the years she had spent with her husband in Philadelphia. Although she had never been able to go back to Philadelphia, she talked with real affection about the United States as the land of opportunity. In the 1870s, shortly after her return from Philadelphia, she had both of her children registered as U.S. citizens at the United States Consulate in Munich.

My father and his sister Francisca went to school in Munich. From the beginning he was a brilliant student. In secondary school (the same Wilhelmsgymnasium which I attended 40 years later), he was consistently the top student in his class. He wound up with only one "B" in his record. As we shall see later, I attempted to do him one better but narrowly failed.

While in secondary school, my father did all kinds of odd jobs in order to bring a little extra income into his mother's till. The family nevertheless lived in very modest circumstances.

When my father graduated from secondary school, the principal of his school recommended him to the Paris Rothschilds, who were seeking to hire a private instructor for their son. Father got the job, and for a year or so became part of the household of one of the world's richest families. He then returned to Munich and studied law, becoming a member of the Bar in the course of the 1890s.

His sister Francisca, who later became one of my favorite aunts, married a businessman by the name of Max Loewenthal. Together they ran a successful corset business (corsets being an indispensable part of women's wear at that time). They had three children, a boy and two girls. With all of these cousins I became quite friendly, although they were much older than I. All of these cousins have passed away; one of them became a victim of the Holocaust.

My sister and I will never forget our Uncle (uncle by marriage) Max Loewenthal. He was the greatest storyteller who ever lived. Whenever we visited Aunt Francisca and Uncle Max, we implored him to tell us stories. Spontaneously, without any preparation, he dreamt up perfectly fascinating children's stories, telling them with an incredible innate talent for timing and dramatic effect. Even today, 75 years later, I remember some of the names and turns of phrases that formed part of Uncle Max's fabulous stories. I only wish they had been recorded. His grandchildren, no doubt, could live handsomely off the royalties.

In the 1890s, while he served as a legal trainee, my father met the girl who was to become his wife and my mother. But before going on with my parents' life story, I should record what I know about my mother's family background.

# CHAPTER II

# MY MOTHER AND HER FAMILY

As a child I knew both of my maternal grandparents very well. My maternal grandfather Heinrich Aufhäuser was born in 1842 in a small Bavarian town near the Danube River. About his early life I know virtually nothing. As a young man he moved from the small town where he was born to the city of Munich, where in 1870 he founded the bank bearing his name, a bank that still exists today under the same name of H. Aufhäuser. The family no longer has an interest in the bank, but its present owners still insist on keeping the name of my grandfather, because the bank under that name has acquired a very fine business reputation. The bank recently sent to all of its customers a pamphlet which contains a photograph of its founder. The photograph shows that in addition to being a successful banker he also was an unusually handsome man. I knew him only when he was in his seventies. At that time, his health was not the best. He had suffered several strokes. But he was still able to walk with the help of a cane, and his mind was as clear and alert as ever. I remember visiting him in his office at the bank and many times at his home.

I also remember quite vividly that he took me to an outdoor cafe where he treated me to ice cream and cake. Grandfather, upon whom the Royal Bavarian Government had bestowed the honorary title of Commercial Counselor, was quite famous for his ability to solve arithmetical problems faster than anyone else. When I was three or four years old, I was able to add and subtract like a second-grader, and Grandfather was very proud of that talent of mine. I still remember whenever we met friends of his in the street or at the outdoor cafe he had me exercise my arithmetical talent and always showed great pride in my precocious mathematical ability. My mother was his youngest child and clearly his favorite, and I think that I was his favorite among his seven grandchildren.

Grandfather, although strongly opposed to orthodoxy, was a religious man. Among religious Jews it is regarded as a sign of special divine grace if a person is permitted to die either on a Sabbath or on a high Jewish holiday. Grandfather died in the fall of 1917 on a day that was both a Sabbath and the highest Jewish holiday, the Day of Atonement. He knew that he was going to die and he derived a great deal of consolation from the fact that he was permitted to die on a day thus graced by the Lord. I was almost eight years old at the time, and the notion of death did not have much meaning for me; but I do remember how completely dissolved in tears my mother was when she received the sad news.

About Grandfather's ancestors I know virtually nothing. More is known to me, on the other hand, about the ancestors of my maternal grandmother, who came from a more urban and rather distinguished family. It seems that her ancestors lived for many years in the Franconian town of Ansbach. From my uncle I heard a story about one of Grandmother's ancestors, probably her grandfather who lived in Ansbach at the time of the Napoleonic Wars. When the town was taken over by Napoleon's army, one of the French officers was lodged in the ancestor's house. This French officer attempted to flirt with the rather pretty wife of the ancestor. Our ancestor took a dim view of that and, being a head taller than the Frenchman, took the Frenchman's sword away from the officer and broke it over his knee. The Frenchman, who obviously knew that he had not played a very honorable role, never reported the incident, and the ancestor got away with this insult to Napoleon's army.

Later the family moved to Munich, and Grandmother's father, my great grandfather Anton Berliner, spent all or most of his life in Munich, where Grandmother Rosa Berliner was born in 1850.

Anton Berliner was somewhat given to eccentricity. It is reported, for example, that he owned 200 pairs of shoes. But apart from being an eccentric, he also must have had other more impressive qualities, as will become clear in an instant. It was doing his lifetime, in the first half of the nineteenth century, that the Jews in his native Bavaria were given the civil and political rights of full citizens, and he was the first Jew to be an officer in the Citizens' Militia, an organization similar to our National Guard. In 1848, the year that saw revolutionary outbreaks all over Europe, there were demonstrations in front of the Royal Palace in Munich, and Anton's militia unit was mobilized to protect the Palace. For quite some time, the demonstrators and the militiamen faced each other. We may assume that there was some verbal heckling and perhaps some shouting. In any event, someone in the Palace lost his nerve and sent a command to our ancestor to order his troops to open fire on the demonstrators. If Anton Berliner had obeyed this command from the Palace, and had given the order to shoot, the result would have been terrible and unnecessary bloodshed; but

Anton followed the moral law embedded in his conscience. He never gave the order to open fire.

Needless to say, by disobeying the order from the Palace he took an enormous personal risk; but the story has a happy ending. The demonstrators remained peaceful and eventually went home. In the days which followed the government made some minor political concessions. The rather elderly king abdicated in favor of his politically more skillful son, and the Bavarian Revolution was over. The high official who had issued the belligerent command to the militia apparently realized how foolishly he had acted, and never brought up the question of Anton Berliner's insubordination. Anton lived to a ripe old age, continuing to receive honors and medals from the Royal Government.

Anton's daughter Rosa, my grandmother, married the promising young banker, Heinrich Aufhäuser, around 1870. They had four children: Bertha, Martin, Siegfried and Emma, the latter to become my mother. Mother's childhood was a happy one. She grew up under the eyes of completely devoted parents and enjoyed the company and playfulness of her three siblings, who were close to her in age. She and her sister developed into striking beauties, Bertha a brunette and Mother a blonde.

# CHAPTER III

# MY PARENTS AND MY OWN CHILDHOOD

Mother's birthday was July 3, 1878. In the mid-eighteen-nineties, when Mother was approximately sixteen years old, her sister Bertha got married to a young businessman by the name of August Heilbronner, who happened to be one of my father's closest friends. Father, therefore, was invited to the wedding, and there he met the bride's sister Emma. It was love at first sight. It was only Mother's tender age, plus the fact that Father was still too young to support a family, that delayed their own wedding for several years. They got married on September 5, 1897. It was, and for over 50 years continued to be, a model marriage, based on unconditional and unlimited mutual devotion. They were very different from each other but their temperaments happily complemented each other. Father was strong-willed, energetic, full of physical and nervous energy, enormously talented (especially as a poet), but given to swings of moods and occasionally tending to fly off the handle. Mother was less strong physically, suffering from migraine headaches, but otherwise healthy and upbeat.

Her outstanding characteristic was her never-changing gentleness and kindness; everybody who came into contact with her loved her and truly adored her as a human angel. All those who had the privilege of living near her were surrounded and deeply affected by her ever-present willingness to help and to heal. At the same time she was no dull goody-goody. On the contrary, she had a puckish sense of humor. Her talent to imitate the speech and gestures of other people was such that often the whole family literally fell under the table laughing. Altogether one can say that ours was a family in which there was much banter and laughter, and this attracted many friends-old and young-into our house.

When I became old enough to be aware of such things, I noticed that many, if not most, of our relatives and friends had extra-marital affairs and that most of their marriages were rocky, to say the least. By way of contrast, the love and devotion that characterized my parents' marriage stood out as a shining example.

In 1902, their first child was born, my sister Thea, who recently celebrated her 90th birthday. My parents strongly desired to have a second child, but the little good-for-nothing kept them waiting for a long time. When the good-for-nothing made his appearance on October 11, 1909, he was named Rudolf Berthold Schlesinger (his middle name Berthold, as has been mentioned, having been the first name-of his long-deceased paternal grandfather).

I am told that as an infant I was fat and an unmitigated pain. My principal occupation apparently was to poke holes into the heads of my sister's dolls. This did not endear me to my sister, and it is truly a miracle that later on we became very close friends.

At this point I should perhaps describe the Schlesinger household in those days of my early childhood. My parents were not rich, but comfortably off – members of the upper-middle class. Life for members of that class was in some ways less comfortable than it would be today, but in other ways much more comfortable. Of course, we had no car. This was before the days of automatic gear-shifts and automatic starters; thus driving a car was very difficult, and only the super-rich who could afford a chauffeur could even think of owning a car. Also there were no dish washers, washing machines, and electric refrigerators. It was not until I was about eight years old that we had central heating; until then it was just a stove in every room, and in the winter that stove had to be serviced every day. On the other hand, we had two servants, a cook and a chambermaid. The latter also performed many of the functions of a nanny. My mother thus did not have to perform any menial household chores, and my parents' social life was not handicapped by the presence of infants in their household; there were two built-in baby sitters in the household itself.

As Mother treated the servants with her usual kindness, they tended to stay with us for long periods of time. Indeed, most of them left us only when they got married. When I was an infant, our chambermaid – nanny was a red-headed Bavarian girl by the name of Maxilmiliane, called Maxi. She and me became fast friends, and she spoiled me in the most unconscionable manner.

Whenever my parents said No to any of my requests, however unreasonable, Maxi would secretly comply with my wishes.

Maxi was a devout Catholic and often took me to her church, with the result that in my earliest days I learned much more about the Catholic religion than about Judaism.

In the spring of 1915, when I was five-and-a-half years old, Maxi left our service in order to get married. This was the first real crisis in my life. I thought I could prevent her leaving by throwing a fit, and when she actually left the house, I locked myself in my room, and for a long time refused to open the door.

Our family remained friendly with Maxi and her family after her marriage. Her husband was a tailor. On weekends I often visited them and their two children in their tiny, very modest apartment. Every year I brought Christmas presents to Maxi and her family, and she never failed to come to our house on Mother's birthday. After World War II we sent CARE packages to Maxi and her family; but she died in the late 1940s. Her son Richard Losert, who with his wife lives in Munich, has remained a friend until this day.

Maxi's successor was a very young and attractive girl by the name of Afra. Still shaken by Maxi's departure, at first I refused to have anything to do with Afra, but soon she won me over, and in the end she became a lifelong friend of my sister and myself. She again stayed with us until she got married in 1920. While she was with us, she virtually was a member of the family. After her marriage we remained good friends. In her old days, when she was widowed, my sister and I frequently visited her in Munich and we supplemented her limited income by a small pension.

As I have said before, my childhood home on the whole was a very happy one. But that happiness came very close to being totally destroyed by tragedy when I was only one year old. In 1910 my parents, who were enthusiastic bicyclists, went on one of their frequent bicycle trips in the Alps. They took along my cousin Fritz Heilbronner (the oldest son of my mother's sister), who was then about 15 years old. They pushed their bicycles up the north side of the Brenner Pass and then gleefully coasted down south in the direction of Bozen (now Bolzano). In the course of this downward ride Mother lost control of her bike which went faster and faster until finally she-was thrown off, falling against a rock. She hit her head and suffered a severe concussion. Father and our cousin Fritz were riding behind her and had to look on helplessly as the accident happened. She had to spend a long time at the hospital, but in the end, fortunately, made a complete recovery.

The earliest concrete event that I can remember goes back to the summer of 1913. The family (including Maxi) spent a month in Lengenfeld, a beautiful village in the Oetztal, a part of Tirol. We occupied a whole floor in a large farmhouse. The farmers' own quarters and the stables were below us, on the ground floor. We had a small kitchen of our own, where Maxi prepared breakfast and lunch for us; for dinner we always went to the local inn. Father spent much of his time trout fishing in the nearby mountain streams. As his helper he took along my sister, who at that time was almost 11. As I was less than four years old, I was considered too young for such a function. To my mind, this was unjustifiable discrimination; but I had no choice in the matter and I had to spend most of my time playing (with or without Maxi) in the yard behind the farmhouse, hereby learning much about the habits of chickens, pigs and other animals.

At the end of the yard that was my daily playground, there was a small tool shed, built against the side of a steep, grassy knoll. The top of the knoll was a favorite grazing spot for cows and other animals. One day – and I shall never forget this – a very young calf grazing at the top of the knoll lost its footing and fell down several hundred feet over the side of the knoll. In the course of the fall, which I breathlessly observed, the body of the poor animal gained tremendous speed. It landed on the roof of the tool shed; but the power of the fall was such that the roof caved in and the body of the injured animal fell to the floor of the tool shed. I was the only person who observed the accident, and I quickly ran into the house-to summon help. The farmer and his wife immediately ran to look after the injured calf. Some of their children and servants joined them, and there was great excitement all around. One of the farmer's children was sent out on a bicycle to call the veterinarian, who arrived after a few minutes and thoroughly examined the poor calf. But apparently nothing could be done for the injured animal, and every member of the farmer's family looked as if they had lost a true friend.

The calf was taken away, and my later questions concerning its fate were never answered by the grown-ups.

When I was a little less than six years old, I began going to school – a public school. My parents thought that I should become acquainted with a broad range of contemporaries, and for this reason they preferred the public elementary school to a private school. The German elementary school system at that time did not provide for a kindergarten class. Thus I started my school life by entering first grade at the Gebele Schule in the Bogenhausen suburb of Munich. There was no transportation, by bus or otherwise; children had to walk to schools. As the school was approximately two miles from our home, this gave me plenty of exercise. On Wednesdays and Saturdays there was school only in the mornings; but on other weekdays the class met mornings and afternoons. No lunch was served at the school. The children had to walk home for lunch and then walk back to school for their afternoon classes. Thus on weekdays other than Wednesdays and Saturdays I had to walk about eight miles a day, undoubtedly a great contribution to my health.

Extolling truth over modesty, I must report that in the first grade as well as in subsequent years I was always the top student in the class. In elementary school the only serious competition came from a pretty girl named Erika. In this way I learned at a tender age that when it comes to brainpower there is no difference between men and women, and this early insight may be one of the reasons why I have always remained free of male chauvinism.

One of my classmates, named Theodore (Dory) Schuessler, was an unprepossessing, red-haired hunchback. The other children tended to tease and occasionally to attack him. I became quite outraged when I witnessed those attacks and tried to protect the poor hunchback. As I was one of the bigger boys in our class, my attempts to protect our unfortunate classmate were quite successful, and he and I became close friends. We regularly played together after class. But after the third grade I left elementary school. From then on my friend and I went to different schools and we drifted apart. Many years later I heard, to my consternation, that he had become an ardent Nazi.

Beginning at the time I was seven years old, my family spent many summers in Fischhausen, an idyllic village located on the shore of a lovely lake in the Bavarian Alps. We always rented the upper floor-of a farmhouse, where we kept house during the summer months. Father was usually too busy to be with us during the whole summer vacation; but as Fischhausen was only a couple of hours by train from Munich, he usually joined us for weekends. I became friendly with the farmers' children and together with them participated in many of the farming chores. On a farm there is plenty of work to do for children. They can feed the chickens. They take the cows to their grazing places and bring them back when it is time for them to be milked. After the grownups cut the grass, it is for the children to rake it and turn it so it can become good dry hay. In these and countless other farming chores I participated, and by the end of each summer I was hardly distinguishable, by speech or manners from the genuine farmers' children.

Every year it was with real regret that at the end of the fun-filled farming summer I went back to school. Speaking of school, I should perhaps say a word about my religious education. In Germany at that time "religion" was a compulsory subject in the elementary and secondary schools. There were separate classes, for Catholics, Protestants and Jews. Since Jewish pupils were a relatively small minority, it was apparently impossible to hold Jewish "religion" classes in every school. Thus the "religion" classes had to be combined for a number of schools, with the result that the place where those classes were taught was quite distant from our house. For this reason my parents petitioned the school authorities for permission to conduct my first grade religious education at home. The permission was granted, and as a result it was my Dad who introduced me to the subject of Biblical History.

The involvement of my Dad in this religious activity calls for a word of exclamation. As I have mentioned before, my maternal grandparents, although opposed to orthodoxy, were religious people and upheld Jewish traditions. My Dad, on the other hand was a convinced atheist. Long and thorough study of the works of secular, philosophers from Plato to Kant, Hegel and Marx had led him to reject religion. He believed in, and lived by, the highest ethical values and commands; but he remained firmly convinced that those values and commands were not rooted in religion. Thus it was difficult for him to teach "religion" to his son, but he brilliantly extracted himself from this dilemma. He taught me biblical history as history, and he did a masterful job. Whatever I know of biblical history I owe much more to his teaching me during my earlier school years than to later studies with professional teachers of "religion." At the beginning of the first grade, when I was not yet able to read, he told me the stories of Abraham and Joseph and David. Later, when I knew how to read, he gave me relevant reading assignments, and we devoted our "class-time" on Sunday mornings to a thorough discussion of what I had read. I have never had a better teacher.

On August 1, 1914, approximately one year before I entered first grade, World War I had begun. The impact of the war on our family was not as immediate or as dramatic as one might think. The German authorities knew that Father had been born in Philadelphia, and they must have realized that consequently he and the members of his family were American citizens. Since his father had been a Prussian subject, they probably treated him as a dual-citizen; but he had never served in the German army. In wartime, the German army perhaps would have attempted to draft him if he had been the right age. Nobody was drafted, however, who had reached the age of 45, and Father, most fortunately, celebrated his 45th birthday just a few weeks after the outbreak of the war.

Father's younger law partner did have to serve in the German army during the war years, with the result that during all those years Father carried a double workload. He never complained about it; but the strain of inordinately long working hours did make itself felt.

Of our closest friends and relations only two were drawn into front-line service. My cousin Fritz Heilbronner (who has been mentioned before) was 19 years old when the war broke out; he served as a paramedic during the whole war but was never injured and was able to embark on the study of medicine as soon as the war was over. Mother's closest friend, Irma Heilbronner (not related to Fritz Heilbronner or to us, but my sister and I called her "Aunt Irma"), who had lost her husband under tragic circumstances just about a year before the beginning of the war, volunteered to become a nurse, and during the whole war served in army hospitals located right in the combat zone. As I shall have to record later, the Nazis rewarded her for that heroic volunteer service by gassing her to death.

During the first two years of the war, life on the home front remained relatively unchanged. But as the years 1916 and 1917 rolled around, the Allied blockade of Germany made itself felt quite drastically. Food and fuel had to be rationed. The rations became ever more skimpy, and many types of food were no longer available at all. For several months even potatoes – our main staple – disappeared from the shelves. Many people suffered from malnutrition. Our family was saved from that fate by two fortunate circumstances: one of Father's clients operated a wholesale cheese business; he paid Father's bills by delivering substantial quantities of cheese – a commodity which otherwise would have been unavailable. The second circumstance that saved us from starvation was that we spent the summer months on a farm where food was plentiful. Thus we were able to fatten ourselves for a couple of months every year, making up for the deprivations suffered during the other months.

School buildings in those days were heated by coal. In the winter of 1916 and 1917, which was unusually cold, Germany suffered such a cruel shortage of coal that for two or three months all schools had to be closed. For us children, of course, this was a cause for rejoicing. In the frigid weather of that winter all lakes were solidly frozen; thus the enforced vacation offered us unlimited opportunities for skating.

In general, however, life in Germany became rather grim during those final years of World War I, and it was not too surprising that in the fall of 1918 the German people's will to fight was exhausted.

# CHAPTER IV

# THE YEARS AT THE GYMNASIUM

In September 1918, about two months before the end of the war, I entered the Wilhelmsgymnasium, the same secondary school from which Father had graduated several decades earlier. Under the system which prevailed in Germany at that time, those students who aspired to university study normally entered the gymnasium (secondary school) after four years of elementary school; but in exceptional cases it was possible to be admitted to the gymnasium after three years of elementary school. My third grade teacher suggested that I skip the fourth grade and go to the gymnasium right after completing the third grade. My parents agreed, but in order to enter the gymnasium directly from third grade, I had to take an examination – the first serious examination of my life. I passed and thus became one of the youngest students ever to attend the Wilhelmsgymnasium.

The academic year 1918–19, my first year at the gymnasium, was filled with many dramatic events that were unconnected with school life. In November 1918, Germany having been defeated in the War, the German Emperor and all the local kings and potentates, including the King of Bavaria, were overthrown. The Weimar Republic was born by way of revolution, and new republican governments were installed at the state as well as the federal level. The central government in Berlin was dominated by moderate social-democrats such as Ebert and Scheidemann. In Bavaria, however, a somewhat more radical wing of the socialists came to power under the leadership of Kurt Eisner, who was an intellectual ideologue but was generally regarded as a man of integrity and sincerity. In the early months of 1919 Eisner was assassinated by Count Arco, the scion of a well-known family of Bavarian aristocrats. In response to this murder, the most radical wing of leftists (they called themselves Spartakists) took over the Bavarian government, and there ensued a reign of terror in which there was grave danger for the lives and the property of all non-leftist citizens. Hoodlums purporting to act on behalf of the government searched homes and businesses, stealing whatever seemed to be of value. My Uncle Martin Aufhäuser, who after my Grandfather's death had become the owner and chief executive of the Aufhäuser Bank, was afraid that the bank's safe deposit boxes might be raided in this way. He tried to hide some of the cash and securities in the basement of his home, which was in the same street as our house. On second thought, however, he regarded that hiding place as not too safe. It occurred to him that our house might be a little safer because my Father, although not a Marxist, was known to have political views that were slightly left of center.

Thus in the dead of night my Uncle and my Father carried suitcases full of cash and securities from my Uncle's home to our house. It was a distance of only a quarter of a mile, but the suitcases were so heavy that the two men were quite exhausted when they arrived at our house, where they stuffed the suitcases into the most ingeniously selected hiding places. I do not think that our family ever had so much wealth under its own roof. Fortunately, nobody came to search or raid our house, and when the reign of terror was over, all the hidden property was transported back to the bank, much to the relief of my parents.

The Spartakists proclaimed Bavaria to be a sovereign Soviet Republic, thereby severing the ties between the Bavarian government in Munich and the central government in Berlin. The Federal government, in order to prevent the immediate breakup of the German Reich, was forced to take strong counter-measures. Under the circumstances, those counter-measures could only be of a military nature. Tragically, therefore, the social-democratic government in Berlin found itself compelled to form a political alliance with what was left of the Imperial German Army. It was that alliance which from the beginning of the Weimar Republic vested overwhelming political power in the generals of the Wehrmacht. History records that later on-in 1933-the generals' influence was one of the main factors in Hitler's takeover of the German-government.

In 1919, the alliance between the Berlin government and the generals had the immediate effect of mobilizing considerable military forces for the fight against the Spartakists in Munich. Those forces consisted partly of regular army units, i.e. the remnants of units that had fought in the war, and partly of so-called volunteer corps. The latter were formed by anti-leftist officers and men who had been demobilized but were willing to resume military duty for a short time in order to preserve German unity which was threatened by the Spartakist insurrection.

The army which thus moved against the Munich insurrectionists was generally referred to as the White Army, or simply "The Whites." Both its regular units and the volunteer corps consisted of war-tested, experienced soldiers, equipped with formidable weaponry.

The Spartakists, although many of their followers were armed, fully realized that in a military showdown they could not possibly prevail against, the White Army. In this predicament, they hit on a desperate idea. They arrested dozens of the city's wealthiest and most prominent citizens and let it be known that those citizens were being held as hostages. The threat was made that if the White Army should make any attempt to occupy Munich, the hostages would be killed.

This turn of events directly and dramatically affected our family. One of our dearest friends and relatives, Bernhard Neuburger, was among the hostages. The reader of these Memoirs will remember Raphael Kraemer, who was a brother of my paternal Grandmother. Raphael had several sons (about whom we shall hear more in the course of this tale) and one daughter by the name of Bertha, who was nicknamed Moppi. Bertha (Moppi) Kraemer, who was my Father's first cousin, married Father's close childhood friend, Bernhard Neuburger. My parents and the Neuburgers were the closest of friends throughout their lives, and the friendship spilled over into the next generation. Thus it was a terrible blow to every member of my own family to learn that Bernhard's life was in such immediate danger. Father, using whatever leftist connections he had, tried desperately to get Bernhard released – but to no avail.

As the White Army moved closer and closer to Munich, the Spartakists threats to do away with the hostages became louder and ever more credible. Needless to say, the leaders of the White Army were not deterred by those threats. As the White Army entered the outskirts of the city, more than a dozen of the hostages were shot dead by the Spartakists. As it turned out, Bernhard was not among those killed; but for several days, until the remaining hostages were liberated by the White Army, his family and his friends were completely in the dark concerning his fate, torn by doubt and fearing the worst.

Why Bernhard was spared when many of his fellow hostages were killed, has never become entirely clear; but it may have had something to do with the fact that he was, and was known to be, an unusually charitable person. It seems likely that one of the Spartakists who selected the hostages to be killed, directly or indirectly was a past beneficiary of Bernhard's charity. Thus charity, for once, may have saved the donor's life.

The Spartakists, lacking heavy weapons, were unable to prevent the White Army from entering the city. But once the Whites were in the city, they encountered dangerous resistance by snipers, and those neighborhoods where there was a heavy concentration of workers had to be conquered by house-to-house fighting. There were heavy casualties on both sides.

While fighting was still going on, the White Army command issued a decree authorizing White Army units to search every house for weapons, and further providing for the most summary trial and execution of every adult male inhabitant of any house in which unauthorized weapons were found. As a result of these house to house searches many rifles and other weapons were uncovered. Hundreds of inhabitants of the houses in question were subjected to drumhead court-martial proceedings presided over by White Army officers. Most of these proceedings resulted in death sentences which were immediately executed. The wives and other family members of the court martial defendants desperately tried to find lawyers to defend them. Most lawyers, however, wanted to have nothing to do with the defense of alleged Spartakists. Father was one of the very few willing to appear, and to represent defendants, before the summary courts-martial. For several weeks, this kept him busy from early morning until late into the night – to the point of total exhaustion. Sometimes he handled as many as 20 such trials in one day. He was, of course, unable to detract from the severity of the decree under the terms of which those summary trials were held; but he was impressed with the fairness of most of the officers who presided over the trials, and he was able to save the majority of his clients from the death penalty.

The White Army, meanwhile, had to find quarters for its officers and men. A young lieutenant from Stuttgart came to live in our house for several weeks. He seemed rather anxious to impress my sister, who was a vivacious 16-year-old at the time. When my sister heard that he belonged to a cavalry unit, she expressed an interest in horseback riding. The lieutenant immediately sent for his horse and gave my sister a chance to ride around in our garden. The effect on our lawn (in which Father always took enormous pride) was quite disastrous, and when Father came home, both my sister and the lieutenant had hell to pay.

Meanwhile, a certain amount of sniping and fighting continued in several parts of the city. The sight of corpses lying in the street became a matter of routine. A handyman who often came to our house to help with the heating and other chores told us proudly that he had been hired by the city government to collect bodies in the street and to transport them to cemeteries. His rate of pay was two marks per body, and I still remember that one day he appeared at our house beaming gleefully and telling us that morning he had already made 22 marks.

After a few weeks, the Spartakists' resistance began to break down, and sniping became more sporadic; but one sniping incident came very close to home. The houses on our street faced the Isar River; but between the river-and our street there was a very pretty public park. Thus there were houses on only one side of the street, with the park on the other side. The trees and bushes of the park provided excellent cover for would-be snipers, and indeed one day a group of perhaps a dozen armed Spartakists hid in the greenery. When a White Army unit came along, the Reds suddenly opened fire. The Whites, of course, immediately returned the fire. Being vastly outnumbered, the snipers ultimately were wiped out. Many of the bullets exchanged in that fight hit our house. For some reason (probably because it was lunchtime) all family members as well as our two servants were at home at the time. As the shootout occurred no more than 50 meters from our house, the noise of battle was quite considerable. Father immediately ordered everybody to lie down flat on the floor, as far as possible away from the front windows. Everybody obeyed the order, except Afra, who was a somewhat adventurous girl and to whom fear was totally unknown. She raced toward the nearest front window in order to get a good view of the action. She did not quite reach the front window, however, because Father shouted at her with such ferocity that even Afra had to obey. I do not think that I have ever heard a human being yell at another at the level of decibels that Father reached at that moment. And a good thing it was. If he had not stopped Afra from getting to the window, she would have been in very real danger of becoming a victim of the shootout. In the street outside our house there were numerous victims, and our friend the handyman made quite a bit of money that day.

When all these vivid impressions of revolution and civil war were thrust upon me, I was only 9 years old. But I was already an avid reader, and the small segment of history and of human and social drama that I had seen with my own eyes further increased my appetite for books, especially those which factually or fictionally dealt with history. My own early experiences helped me to see and to understand the human element that is ever-present in historical processes, and in subsequent years the great historical plays, especially those by Shakespeare and Schiller, became my favorite reading. Inspired by such reading, I also tried my own hand at writing plays as well as poetry.

After the final collapse of the Spartakist insurrection, in the Spring of 1919, Bavaria was reintegrated into the German Reich, and until the attempted Hitler Putsch of 1933 (about which a word will be said below) I experienced no further revolutionary excitement. The worldwide flu epidemic, which in late 1918 and throughout the year 1919 killed many of its victims (especially young adults), caused much fear but did not hit our own family and friends.

For our family, the big event of the year 1920 was the return to Munich of Mother's brother Siegfried Aufhäuser, whom we children called "Uncle Siegl." Thereby hangs a tale of events that turned out to be of central significance in my own adult life: the birth of the friendship between our family and the Hirschlands.

To explain it all, I must start at the beginning. As a very young man, Siegfried left his parents' Munich home and migrated to London, where in time he became a successful stockbroker. He remained a bachelor and was rumored to be exceptionally popular with members of the opposite sex. By naturalization he became a British subject and probably intended to make London his permanent home. But when World War I broke out in 1914, England was gripped by a fierce outbreak of anti-German hysteria. Suspicion of everything German extended even to British subjects of German extraction. Every German-born British subject was asked to sign a declaration condemning and vilifying his native country; those who refused to sign the declaration were expelled from Britain and all their property was confiscated. Siegfried did not sign the declaration. Thus he had to leave Britain, at least for the duration of the war, and he decided to spend the war years in neutral Sweden. As his property in England was confiscated, he had to lead a very modest life in Sweden; but he learned the Swedish language and spent most of his time in a small village where he engaged in much skiing and, it was rumored, in multiple amorous activities. When the war was over, he returned to London. The British authorities did not question his continuing British citizenship, but he encountered much difficulty in trying to recover his property, which had been confiscated by the British government at the beginning of the war. Finally, however, after lengthy legal proceedings, and with the help of an excellent lawyer, he got all of his property back. This happened in 1920. At that point he was free to start a new business career at any place of his choosing. His brother Martin, who after Grandfather's death had become the sole owner of the Aufhäuser Bank, invited him to become a partner. Accepting that invitation, Siegfried returned to Munich and became a partner in the bank. At about the same time the two brothers took in a third partner, a lawyer by the name of Emil Kraemer (not a relative), about whom much will be said later on.

After his return to Munich Siegfried at first lived with his mother, Grandmother Aufhäuser. As he was a man of great generosity as well as charm and loved to spoil his nieces and nephews, his return was a most joyful event for us children. Very wisely, as it turned out, he retained his British citizenship. Due to his Swedish connections and his knowledge of the Swedish language, he was appointed Honorary Consul, later Consul General, of the Kingdom of Sweden.

The Aufhäuser Bank by that time had become one of Germany's prominent private banking firms. Another outstanding private bank was the Simon Hirschland Bank in Essen, which at that time was owned by the third generation of Hirschland bankers, the brothers Kurt and Georg Hirschland. It so happened that Kurt's mother-in-law, who was the widow of another German banker and lived in Duesseldorf, was British-born and had considerable property in England. Since she had been married to a German and was living in Germany, all of that property was confiscated by the British government at the beginning of World War I. When in 1920 Kurt Hirschland heard through the grapevine that his fellow banker Siegfried Aufhäuser had been successful in recovering his confiscated British property, he got in touch with Siegfried, asking for advice as to what to do about the confiscated property of his mother-in-law. Siegfried, whose willingness and desire to help other people was one of his outstanding traits, immediately responded. Although the Hirschlands at that time were only superficial acquaintances, he promptly took a train to Essen and spent several days there, giving Kurt Hirschland the benefit of his (Siegfried's) experience with the complicated legal procedures by which such confiscated property might be recovered. The end result was that Kurt's mother-in-law in fact recovered all of her property, and – more importantly – that a deep and lasting friendship between the Hirschlands and our family was born. That friendship spawned two happy marriages, including that of Ruth Hirschland and Rudolf B. Schlesinger – but I am getting ahead of myself; this will be the stuff of later chapters.

At the gymnasium meanwhile I continued the study of Latin and other learned subjects and developed a strong interest in playing soccer. One attractive feature of the Wilhelmsgymnasium was that it was located only a few minutes from my Grandmother's apartment. Thus, whenever I had a free hour between classes I would march over to visit Grandmother, and she and her housekeeper Greti, who was a great friend of mine, would never fail to treat me to cookies, baked apples and other goodies. As I became more mature, a genuine adult friendship developed between Grandmother and me. We shared our problems. On innumerable occasions, Grandmother's advice helped me in solving my problems, and as I grew up, I may have been able occasionally to help her with hers. At the same time, we had much fun together. Surely it was Grandmother who laid the groundwork for my large collection of Jewish jokes. In her last years, she was plagued by eye troubles and other health problems, and I was able to be of some assistance accompanying her (by streetcar) when she had to see one of her doctors.

Every wine connoisseur knows that 1921 was an extraordinary vintage, the reason being that throughout Europe the summer of 1921 was unusually sunny and hot. Our family spent that summer in the Zillertal, an alpine valley in Tirol. That summer my parents did not rent a farmhouse; we stayed in a lovely country inn. Because of the heat, however, we tried to spend as much time as possible at higher altitudes, where hikers were rewarded by cool mountain air. For part of the summer we were joined by Mother's friend Irma Heilbronner (Aunt Irma), whom I have mentioned before. I particularly remember one mountain trip taken by the five of us – the four Schlesingers and Aunt Irma. Our plan was to hike to the Rerliner Huette, a fairly large refuge located high up in the mountains and facing a large glacier. That glacier was a famous tourist attraction because at its entrance there was an ice cave reputed to be one of the largest of its kind in the entire Alps.

After a day of fairly strenuous climbing we arrived at the refuge in the late afternoon, only to be told that all the rooms were already occupied. Thus we had no choice but to spend the night in a nearby hayloft – much to my delight, although the grown-ups perhaps were a little less delighted. Everybody, however, slept well, and the next morning, after a healthy breakfast at the refuge, we climbed up the short distance to the entrance of the famous ice cave. The outside temperature was unusually warm, considering it was early in the morning and we were high up in the mountains. It was quite a relief, therefore, to get into the cave, where it was beautifully cool. As the cave was very large, there was plenty of opportunity for walking around and for admiring the blue sheen on the grandiose walls of ice all around. The bottom of the cave was quite wet, and one had to skip from rock to rock, which my sister and I enjoyed a great deal. Everybody had a good time, and under normal circumstances we probably would have spent most of the morning in the cool and lovely cave. But after five or ten minutes Mother suddenly began nagging us to get out of the cave. This was most surprising. There was no rational reason for leaving the cool cave and going back into the hot sunshine; and as the reader knows, Mother was certainly not the nagging type. On this occasion, however, she seemed quite transformed. Gone was her usual gentleness, and with uncommon insistence, in an almost nasty manner, she forced us to leave the cave in a hurry. Father, who by nature was not usually submissive, apparently was so surprised and impressed by Mother's abrasive insistence that, though grumbling, he complied with Mother's wishes; so did Aunt Irma, my sister and I. After we had left the cave, Mother – again insistently – made us descend fairly rapidly toward the refuge. When we were about 500 meters from the cave we suddenly heard a thunderous noise above us. When we looked up, we saw a massive ice avalanche coming down the glacier. It traveled at a tremendous and accelerating speed in the direction of the cave. When the avalanche, which must have weighed hundreds or perhaps thousands of tons, reached the top of the cave, the noise became an overpowering roar, and the whole cave – perhaps weakened by a lengthy period of unusually hot weather – collapsed under the crushing weight of the avalanche. As we had been there just a few minutes before, we knew that there were people in the cave. We rushed to the refuge in order to summon help. Before we arrived there, however, trained Alpinists were already on their way up to the cave-or what had been the cave – in order to save the people who had been trapped in the disaster. But the masses of ice occupying the space of the former cave proved impenetrable, and it turned out to be impossible to extricate any of the victims. While we watched the hopeless efforts to save the unlucky ones, we had plenty of time to reflect on the grace of fate – or The Lord – which through Mother's sixth sense had spared the five of us from being buried under tons of ice.

The next year – 1922 – was the beginning of my lifelong passion for bicycling. The reason my parents, who were enthusiastic bicyclists, had kept me from bicycling until I was 12 years old, probably was that they had become overly cautious as a result of Mother's near-fatal bicycling accident which I have mentioned above. In early 1922, however, I was given a shiny new bicycle (grown-up size), and my beloved Uncle Moritz, one of Father's cousins and a brother of Moppi Neuberger, taught me how to ride a bike.

Uncle Moritz had a daughter but no son. Ever since the days of my early childhood, he and I got along wonderfully and he became almost a second father of mine. He, like his father Raphael, was in the business of selling raw skins to tanneries. Many of his customers were in villages and small towns all over central, southern and southeastern Europe. As suitable transportation facilities were largely absent in those days, he depended on his bicycle for visits to his customers, and indeed he had bicycled many thousands of miles across the highways and byways of a large part of Europe. But his enthusiasm for bicycling was such that when he took a vacation, he spent it – you guessed it – bicycling over every mountain pass in the Alps, often in the company of my parents. Needless to say, the bicycles of those days had only one speed; thus an up-hill trip meant either pushing your bike or using your muscles very hard.

With all this experience, Uncle Moritz of course was a splendid bicycle instructor. Under his tutelage I made such rapid progress that in the summer of 1922 Father took me along on a wonderful bicycle trip through Tirol and Vorarlberg – the first of many such Alpine excursions. The other participants in that particular venture were my sister (age 19) and one of her admirers by the name of Hans. We had quite a few scary experiences. One that sticks in my mind occurred while we were riding from Zuers to Lech. Both of these places are now famous ski resorts; but in 1922 they were remote and fairly unknown villages, located in the midst of grandiose scenery but connected only by a footpath. As we rode down that path from Zuers to Lech, there was a steep mountain to the right and an even steeper precipice to our left. We rode with appropriate caution, but my sister's rear wheel apparently got stuck on the muddy road and she fell off the bike. Being exceedingly skillful and athletic, she managed to throw herself to the right side of the path, thus avoiding the precipice to our left. But her bike fell down the precipice with a terrible clatter. My sister, fortunately, was unhurt. Her bike, however, could be seen 200 meters down the precipice, where its further fall had been prevented, by a tree. Her friend Hans, who had been hardened by four years of front-line service in the war, volunteered to climb down and salvage the bike, which indeed he did, to his everlasting glory. (My sister was duly impressed, but not sufficiently to marry him, as it turned out later.)

In the same year – 1922 – I gave my first public speech. The occasion was, of course, my Bar Mitzvah. During the service, I had to recite a long Hebrew prayer. Since I did not completely trust my ability to read Hebrew from a text without vowels, I had taken the precaution of learning it by heart. What I liked much better, however, was the opportunity given to me for making a speech. I do not remember what I said; but my Grandmother – with that objectivity for which grandparents are so justly famous – decided authoritatively that it was a great speech. As my Bar Mitzvah present, she gave me a leather suitcase, which was of such superior quality that I was able to use it for over 50 years.

Nobody who lived in Germany during the years 1922 and 1923 will ever forget the impact of those years' ruinous inflation. Things that used to cost one mark, would rise in price to tens and hundreds and thousands of marks, and finally to millions, billions, and trillions. The value of money changed so rapidly that businesses had to pay their employees daily. When the employees got their pay in the course of the morning, they immediately rushed out to spend the money for food and other necessities, knowing that in the afternoon the same amount of money would buy only a small fraction of what it bought in the morning.

We spent the summer of 1923 in our favorite farmhouse in Fischhausen. Once or twice a week I bicycled to Schliersee, the nearest larger village, with a knapsack full of paper money representing millions and billions of marks, to do the marketing for the family. The food which I brought home in the same knapsack weighed only a little more than the money which it replaced.

For a budding young mathematician, food prices running into the billions and trillions were an exhilarating challenge. But the social consequences of this destruction of monetary values were grave. A large portion of the middle class lost all of their savings. It is hard to fathom the depth of the political resentment caused by this development. If one suffers a disastrous loss as the result of robbery or of taxation, one knows at least how it all happened. But to lose one's entire fortune due to inflation, is quite different. One does not even know what has happened; it is like the work of an invisible hand that has emptied one's pockets. In the case of the great German inflation, the resentment of the victims was further aggravated by the fact that the financial disaster did not hit everybody alike. Those whose fortunes consisted of savings accounts, war bonds, or other bonds, were totally wiped out. Those, on the other hand, who had invested their money in stocks or real property, were essentially spared. Some people even profited from inflation, by buying property, especially real property, with borrowed funds, which subsequently could be repaid by using devalued paper money.

The rage of those expropriated by inflation was one of the important factors – though not the only one – in the rise of Nazism. It is certainly no accident that Hitler's first attempt to seize power occurred on November 9, 1923, at the very height of the inflationary spiral (and, incidentally, just about a week before the period of inflation ended on the day when the German Central Bank created a new currency by converting one trillion old marks into one new mark). Hitler's attempted power grab, the so-called Beer Hall Putsch, took the form of a march of the Nazis and their followers into the center of Munich. When they reached the center, they came up against some units of State Police. Thinking that those in command of the State Police were in sympathy with them, and that consequently the police would not seriously oppose them, the Nazis kept on marching toward the police units. But the Nazis' confidence in the sympathetic attitude of the police proved to be misplaced. The police opened fire, and some of the Nazi marchers were killed. This was the end of their march to power, at least for the time being. Hitler was arrested and tried; but as history records, the Bavarian court treated him with unconscionable leniency.

Again, as in 1919, the civil war struck close to home. This time there were no bullet holes in the walls of our house. The shooting took place almost two kilometers from where we lived. But it so happened that Mother went to see her furrier that very morning. As the furrier's shop was only 200 meters from the place of the shooting, she was uncomfortably close to the action. Fortunately, however, she got home unhurt.

As this was before the age of television, or even radio, it took some time for the news to get around. It was not until the next day that we learned of the complete failure of Hitler's putsch. Until then, all kinds of rumors of ongoing revolutionary action were flying around. A close friend of ours, Dr. Otto Pflaum, who was Honorary Consul of Spain, invited us to spend night in his apartment, suggesting that as the home of a consul (with a nice consular emblem on the door) it might be safer than our house in the event of a Nazi takeover. We gratefully accepted his invitation and spent the night on sofas and easy chairs in Dr. Pflaum's apartment. I slept soundly, but the same was not true of other members of the family. The next day, some newspapers appeared and brought the welcome news of the collapse of the putsch. Thus we were able to thank our friend for his hospitality and to go home.

At this point, I should perhaps say a few words about our friend Dr. Pflaum. He was a lawyer, but his interests were not really focused on the law. As he had spent quite a bit of time in Spain, and spoke Spanish fluently, he was approached by the publisher of the largest Munich newspaper and was asked to become the editor of a weekly magazine to be published in Spanish. The idea was to appeal to readers in Spain and Latin America who were interested in German culture. Dr. Pflaum actually started that magazine, which became quite successful. Later on he was appointed the chief executive of the whole publishing concern, assuming responsibility for Munich's leading newspaper. Politically that paper was slightly right of center, but strongly opposed to Hitler and his cohorts, who published their own newspaper, the Voelkischer Beobachter. Around 1930, at which time the Nazis had become a rather powerful opposition party in the German Parliament, relations between the Voelkischer Beobachter and the leading newspaper became extremely hostile. When the Voelkischer

Beobachter published a viciously libelous article about its rival paper, personally attacking Dr. Pflaum, the latter and his newspaper initiated a libel action. The trial of that action lasted many weeks. During that period, Dr. Pflaum got ill; but defying medical advice, he continued to attend the trial every day. Only when the trial ended, could he be persuaded to go to bed, but by then he had developed a severe Streptococcus infection. Penicillin had not yet been discovered, and within a few days he died, long before his time. In the light of hindsight, however, his fate may have been benign. About two years after his death the Nazis came into power. One hates to think how they would have dealt with him had he still been alive. All of his friends and colleagues who under his leadership had published the leading newspaper were tortured to death in the most beastly manner during the very first weeks of the Nazi regime.

Dr. Pflaum, who was divorced and had no children of his own, became a true paternal friend of mine during my teenage years. It was through him that I got my first paying job: as a part-time proofreader. During my last three or four years at the gymnasium, I used to spend several afternoons a week in the office of his newspaper. There, equipped with a red pencil, I did the same kind of work as the professional proofreaders, and received the same hourly pay – which in terms of a teenager's income amounted to a royal sum. This early proofreading experience has helped me a great deal throughout my life. To this day, when I look at a printed page, the misprints practically leap out of the page. In proofreading my own books and other writings, this has always been a genuine advantage.

1925 stands out in my memory as the year in which I took my first trips to Italy. In the spring of that year, during Easter vacation, my Aunt Francisca and her son Fritz (who was half a generation older than I and had a fairly profound knowledge of Italian art and culture) took me to Venice. All three of us were indefatigable walkers and sightseers, and in looking at innumerable churches, palaces and museums, we became inebriated with the beauty of that unique city. Later in life, often accompanied by my own family, I would return again and again.

The second Italy trip – this one in the summer of 1925 – ended in tragedy. In the early summer of that year my sister had obtained her Ph.D. degree in musicology from the University of Munich. Immediately thereafter the family, in high spirits, left for a summer vacation in Italy. We first stayed a few weeks at a beautiful mountain resort near Bolzano and then traveled to Florence, where we spent the days sightseeing and the evenings tasting exquisite Italian food and wines. After a few days, however, my sister suddenly came down with a severe headache and other symptoms of what we thought was a flu-like illness. On the second or third day of that illness, when she got out of bed in the morning, she fell to the floor, and soon it became apparent that she had no strength whatever in her right leg. The Italian doctor who was quickly summoned, was puzzled and unable to explain her symptoms; but when we got in touch with our physician in Munich he immediately suspected that it was a case of infantile paralysis. On our trip home I had to carry Thea into and out of taxis and railroad cars. As there was no cure for polio, her right leg remained paralyzed for a considerable period of time, and I had to carry her around the house. Later, by intensive physical therapy, she regained minimal use of her right leg; but she has remained severely handicapped all her life. In spite of that handicap, however, and perhaps in part because of it, she has been extraordinarily successful, as will be reported in later parts of this story.

During my last few years at the gymnasium I developed a teenager's normal interest in social life. Tennis and dancing lessons provided an appropriate context.

At the same time – again during the last three or four years at the gymnasium – my academic interests became more intensive and more selective. History and mathematics were my favorite subjects. Within the area of mathematics, I became particularly fascinated by calculus and probability theory. During the academic year 1926–27, my last year at the gymnasium, I had many conversations with my parents concerning the further course of my studies. Under the German system of education, a student is forced to choose her or his career before entering the university i.e. during the last year of study at the gymnasium. The moment a student enters the university, his or her general education is considered complete, and by choosing one of the "faculties" of the university, the student in effect selects a profession and a career. In terms of intellectual interest, my first choice would have been to focus on the study of history; but it was clear that a history graduate could make a living only by teaching history. The idea of teaching history on the secondary school level did not attract me; and to break into a teaching career at the university level, was very difficult in Germany (even during the Weimar Republic) for a Jew.

Similar problems deterred me from becoming a mathematician. I can still hear my father say: "As a mathematics graduate all you can do is teach mathematics." At that time (1926 or 1927) he was undoubtedly right. Neither he nor I foresaw the exponential expansion of career opportunities for mathematicians which later would be brought about by the development of computers.

I was not saddened by the fact that the fields of history and mathematics did not seem to offer inviting career opportunities. There was a third alternative which I found equally attractive: the law. It was not my father who influenced me in that direction. He had been a successful lawyer but not an enthusiastic one. My decision to turn to law as a career was truly my own. Having been brought up in a lawyer's household, and having listened to innumerable conversations about legal theory and legal practice, I had independently developed a very strong interest in the subject. Thus the decision was made that once I was ready to enter the university, I would enroll in the faculty of law. Before I could do so, however, I had to surmount the dreaded hurdle of the "Abitur," the comprehensive examination covering nine years of study at the gymnasium. The grade one receives in the Abitur is composed half of the regular grades accumulated during the last year at the gymnasium, and half of the grades obtained in the examination itself. Thus I was not particularly nervous. My regular grades accumulated during the last year were such that I could not flunk; but of course I was anxious to obtain a first-rate overall result. Just before the examination I caught a bad cold and during the whole examination period I ran a high fever. Nevertheless I did not do too badly; but I did get two Bs, which shattered my ambition to beat my father's record. That I came out number one in my class and number three in the State of Bavaria, was only a small consolation.

# CHAPTER V

# LAW STUDY IN EUROPE

Having passed the "Abitur" in the spring of 1927, I was now a university student. With the approval of my parents I had decided that in order to broaden my outlook and to perfect my French, I should spend my first semester of university study at a French-speaking university. (Under the German system of higher education, a student does not have to take his whole course of study at the same university; he may move around from university to university. For practical reasons, however, it is advisable to spend the last three or four semesters at the place where one takes the final examination.) My choice for the first semester, the summer term 1927, fell on Geneva, Switzerland, and thus at the end of April 1927, I took off for that beautiful city at the Swiss-French border.

In Geneva I stayed with a lovely family that made a living by taking in boarders. The lady of the house probably spoke German and English quite well; but she acted as if she could not understand a word in any language other than French, thus forcing everybody to speak French. As I took all my meals with that family, this gave me plenty of opportunity for improving my French, and when I made mistakes, the lady of the house very graciously would always repeat my sentence in correct form.

This was the first time that I was away from home for an extended period, and I made ample use of that new freedom. The German educational system is characterized by considerable academic pressure at the gymnasium level; but once a student advances to the university, he or she is suddenly given complete "academic freedom", i.e. freedom to study or not to study. In university courses nobody checks on attendance, and a German law student in those days did not have to take any course examinations. It was only at the end of the whole course of study that a comprehensive final examination had to be taken. The result, of course was that youngsters emerging from the gymnasium's atmosphere of pressure into the complete freedom granted by the university did not spend too much of their time on academic pursuits during the early semesters of law study. I was no exception. In fact, at the University of Geneva I did not even enrol in many law courses. The courses in which I enrolled dealt mostly with French literature and political science, and as to attending those courses I used a certain amount of discretion. Thus I had plenty of time for tennis, for a rich social life, and for exploring the beautiful surroundings of Geneva on my bicycle. Playing ping-pong at the International Students' Club, I met fellow students from every part of the world.

Between the two world wars Geneva was the seat of the League of Nations, the international organization which preceded the United Nations. History, of course, records the failure of the League to restrain the aggressive moves of Mussolini, Stalin and Hitler. What is less well remembered is the fact that prior to the wars of aggression started by those dictators and especially in the 1920s, some promising (though in the end unsuccessful) steps towards a lasting peace had been taken under the aegis of the League of Nations. Two great statesmen, Briand in France and Stresemann in Germany, deserved much of the credit for those attempts to turn the League into a true instrument of peace. I was very lucky in that some of the most important meetings of those statesmen – meetings which inspired worldwide hopes for a lasting peace and for true cooperation among nations – took place in Geneva during the few months when I was there. Both Briand and Stresemann liked to meet with students, and thus I had several opportunities for meeting those great men in an informal atmosphere and for asking them questions. Much excitement was generated by what happened at the League of Nations in 1927. We all felt that we were observing the most important and most uplifting events in the history of the world, and that the plague of war would forever disappear from this planet. Little did we know that within the next decade the Japanese would invade Manchuria, and that – also within the next decade – dictators in Italy, Germany and Russia would begin to embark on ugly wars of conquest. My stay in Geneva became memorable also for another, more personal reason: It gave rise to wonderful lifelong friendships. When I set out for Geneva, one of our friends in Munich gave me a letter of introduction to Dr. and Mrs. Jacob Hirsch. Dr. Hirsch was a very successful art dealer, specializing in Greek and Roman art. He was also known to be one of the leading classical archaeologists of his time. He and his wife lived in a lovely mansion, surrounded by a large park in the most beautiful residential area of Geneva. Following the usual ritual, I went there shortly after my arrival on a Sunday morning in order to present my letter of introduction and my visiting card. When I handed those documents to the uniformed maid who opened the door, she informed me that Dr. Hirsch was on a business trip in America, and that Madame was not receiving anybody because she was not well. I had no choice but to leave the letter and the visiting card in the maid's hands and to return home. But as I was walking back through the park, the maid suddenly came running after me and told me that Madame did wish to see me. Thus I entered the mansion and was greeted by Mrs Hedwig Hirsch, a charming lady who was approximately my mother's age. She explained smilingly that she had indeed instructed the maid not to let anybody see her this morning, but that she changed her mind when she saw my name on the visiting card. Why, I asked, did my name mean anything to her? Her answer was astounding. It seems that 13 years earlier, when I was four years old, Mrs. Hirsch was one of a large number of ladies attending a tea party given by my mother at our house in Munich. At one point, I was brought into the room – (probably by Maxi) in order to be exhibited to the assembled ladies. One of the ladies – not my mother – then proceeded to ask me: "Rudi, which of the ladies here is the prettiest?" There is no doubt that my mother was the prettiest; but I probably felt that it would not be appropriate to select her. I am told that I looked around the room for a long time, saying nothing, and that there was real tension among the ladies. Finally after long hesitation, I pointed at one of the ladies and said: "This one". As it happened. "This one" was Mrs. Hirsch, who indeed was a very good-looking woman, and she never forgot the episode. Her telling me the story 13 years later was the beginning of a wonderful generation-spanning friendship with her and her husband (who soon thereafter returned from his trip to New York).

Dr. and Mrs. Hirsch, who had no children of their own, took great delight in spoiling me. In their chauffeur-driven Chrysler they took me to the choicest resorts in the Swiss and French Alps. This was my first step into the world of luxury, compared to which my own family's life-style appeared truly spartan. I still remember a long weekend which we spent at the famous Palace Hotel in the Swiss mountain village of Villars, high above the Rhone Valley. That particular weekend was memorable for two reasons. I won the ping-pong tournament at the Palace Hotel, which gave a lift to my ego. Secondly, and more importantly, it turned out many years later that Putti was in the same hotel at the same time. We did not know each other then. Even if we had known each other it would not have made much difference, as she was seven and I was seventeen!

Nevertheless, we feel that the coincidence of our having been there at the same time is remarkable, especially in view of the fact that Villars later on was to become our and our children's favorite vacation spot.

With one of the many fellow students I met in Geneva I formed a close lifelong friendship. He was Carl Fulda, the son and only child of the famous German playwright, Ludwig Fulda. Carl, like myself, was in his first semester of law study. Our interests, it turned out, were very much the same. Unlike most of our German, English and American fellow students, we were genuinely interested in French culture and in mastering the French language. Carl, as a matter of fact, had a special reason for that interest. His father had become famous for his masterful German translations of the works of Molière and of Rostand's Cyrano de Bergerac, and in recognition of that achievement had been made a member of the French Legion of Honor.

Ultimately, both Carl and I wound up as American law professors. Both of us migrated from Europe to the United States during the 1930s. Thus, although we never lived in the same place, we were able to see each other fairly often, both before and after our emigration from Europe. For me, all those meetings were a source of delight, enlivened by Carl's exceptional sense of humor and by the breadth of his literary and other interests. The friendship lasted until Carl's life was wiped out by cancer in 1976. In September 1927, before returning to Germany, Carl and I took a sightseeing trip through Provence and the French Riviera. That magnificent trip was a fitting climax of the Geneva semester.

The next two terms (winter semester 1927–28 and summer semester 1928) I studied at the University of Munich, beginning to get my teeth into legal subjects. In the spring of 1928 our family got its first car, a rather spiffy convertible. As we did not belong to the class of people employing chauffeurs, Father and I had to learn how to drive. For Father, who was fifty-eight at the time, this was a fairly courageous undertaking. We went to driving school at the same time. Our driving teacher, a retired army sergeant, commented on the fact that I always drove twice as fast as Father, and confidently predicted that my speeding would lead to an early and violent death – a prediction which fortunately did not come true (as a matter of fact I never had an accident during fifty-two years of driving). Father and I both passed the driving examination, and during the ensuing years spent almost every weekend driving through beautiful alpine valleys, many of which we had previously explored as bicyclists.

Another event that occurred during 1928 was my sister's first and very brief marriage. After only four months the marriage fell apart and was followed by divorce. My sister then got a very good job with the Central Music Institute in Berlin, an arm of the Prussian Ministry of Education. She started her new job in the fall of 1928. Thea and I travelled to Berlin together, because I had decided to spend the winter semester 1928–29 at the University of Berlin, and the opening of the semester coincided with the beginning of my sister's job. In Berlin, we lived together for half a year, renting part of an apartment.

At that time Berlin had become the musical and theatrical capital of Europe, and perhaps of the world. Uncle Siegl and Dr. Pflaum, on frequent visits to Berlin, invited us to see the most splendid performances of plays, operas and musicals – performances I shall never forget. At the same time, I began to study law more seriously, inspired by the lectures of truly great scholars such as Martin Wolff, James Goldschmidt and Arthur Nussbaum (all of whom) being Jewish, were kicked out by the Nazis a few years later.

One little adventure which was shared by my sister and me during our joint stay in Berlin was caused by the weather Gods. The winter 1928–29 probably was the coldest ever encountered in Germany. The temperature in Berlin dropped to minus 25° Fahrenheit. The principal fuel used at that time was coal, which normally was transported from Upper Silesia to Berlin by a system of canals. In the winter of 1928–29 those canals froze, and Berliner found themselves without fuel. Our landlady, like everybody else, ran out of coal and our apart merit became unheated. For a few days we froze bitterly, but then the situation was saved by the fact that one of my sister's boyfriends had an uncle who was part-owner of a coal mine in Upper Silesia. That uncle had an office in Berlin, and we were permitted to pick up a sack of coal at that office. I brought that precious commodity home by taxi, and we were able to get our stoves going again for a few hours a day.

The term in Berlin was my fourth semester of law study. For the remaining four semesters I stayed in Munich, where I intended to take the comprehensive examination. During that period (beginning in early 1929) I became more and more enthusiastic about the study of law. Under the influence of brilliant teachers, I developed a particularly intensive interest in Civil Procedure and Commercial Law. The Chair in Civil Procedure at the University of Munich at that time was held by Professor Wilhelm Kisch, whose lectures were so fascinating and amusing that they were always attended not only by law students but also by many other students and by numerous people who were not students at all. Commercial Law was taught by Professor Rudolf Mueller-Erzbach, who was the author of one of the leading treatises on the subject.

In addition to lecture courses, the law faculty offered so-called exercises, in which students were given the opportunity to write papers on the legal implications of complex fact situations. The trouble was that because of the large number of participating students the professors did not have enough time to read and grade those papers; that job was handled by young and relatively inexperienced assistants. In the Commercial Law exercises, however, I was lucky enough to receive a very high grade, with the fortunate result that I was one of the handful of students who were invited to participate in Professor Mueller-Erzbach's seminar. Each seminar participant had to prepare an elaborate seminar paper, which was then discussed at length in one of the seminar sessions. I worked very hard in preparing my paper, which dealt with the somewhat abstruse topic of inchoate legal relationships. Professor Mueller-Erzbach apparently liked my paper and from that time on became an exceedingly kind and attentive supervisor of my studies.

During the last two years of my University law studies I also began to spend some time hanging around my father's law office. Father and his law partner gave me a chance to work on actual cases, especially those involving intricate legal questions. Frequently I came up with bold ideas, and when those ideas were adopted or followed up by Father or his law partner, my ego began to swell. On one occasion this ego-effect became particulary strong. Father had lost an important case in the Intermediate Appellate Court. He asked me to study the Court's opinion and to see whether I could discover a flaw in it. For several days I worked day and night on the case and I finally did discover what I considered a legal flaw. Father agreed with me and using my theory appealed the case to the Supreme Court of Germany. That court also agreed with my theory and reversed the decision of the Intermediate Appellate Court. As I was only a law student at the time, the impact of that victory on my self-confidence was strong and lasting, and my sense of modesty suffered accordingly.

Although I worked hard during those years, I was able to devote some time to extra-curricular activities. I took up horseback riding, and while I never became an accomplished horseman, I did enjoy the many wonderful rides we took on the outskirts of Munich. Two of those rides became potentially dangerous. Once we rode over a meadow adjoining a golf course, and my horse was hit by a golf ball. The speed with which the horse took off was quite considerable, and I had to struggle for several minutes to get the horse under control again; but I managed to stay in the saddle. The second dangerous incident was due to what might be described as a deficiency in my sex education. I was part of a group engaged in a crisp gallop across a vast meadow. My horse was a stallion and I failed to notice that the horse in front of me was a mare. In galloping along we got too close to that mare, and suddenly my horse pulled really close to the mare and rose on his hind legs, throwing me into the meadow. I landed on my shoulder and thought nothing of that little fall at the time; but 30 years later an acute attack of bursitis in that same shoulder reminded me of my amorous stallion.

The summer of 1929 brought me a wonderful opportunity for mountain climbing. The parents of my friend Carl Fulda owned a lovely villa at Karersee (Carezza) in the Italian Alps. They invited me to join them there for a few weeks. Carl and I had done some mountain climbing together two years earlier, when we took off from Geneva to climb some of the peaks in the Mont Blanc area. Now, in 1929, we tackled the beautiful scraggy peaks of the Dolomites. It was an unforgettable experience. At the same time my stay at Karersee gave me an opportunity to get better acquainted with Carl's parents. His father, the famous playwright, was not at all stuffy and indeed turned out to be exceedingly witty. Everybody had an enjoyable and hilarious time. Fortunately, none of us had an inkling that ten years later Carl's father would be driven to suicide by Nazi persecution.

In the summer of 1930 our family, lured by a newspaper advertisement which Mother had spotted, discovered what turned out to be the ideal and indeed perfect vacation spot. It was the tiny fishing village of Salvore, located in Istria on the east coast of the Adriatic Sea, approximately 30 or 40 kilometers south of Trieste. Unmanageable roads made it virtually impossible to get to Salvore by land; but once a day a tiny steamboat went down the Istrian coast from Trieste, and in that way one could reach Salvore quite comfortably but not too speedily. There were no hotels there but only one small pensione run by a very nice Austrian couple. The pensione was located right on the water's edge, and the swimming was superb. A nearby pine forest, provided shade and the most delicious pine fragrance I have ever encountered. The pensione could house only about a dozen guests, an exquisite selection of nature lovers attracted by what may have been the most unspoiled resort in Europe. At that time Istria belonged to Italy, and the fishermen and other inhabitants of Salvore were Italians. There was a tiny post office in the village. To get there from our pensione one had to walk about 20 minutes. After a while my family noticed that I walked there every day, sometimes purchasing only a single postage stamp. When they began to investigate why I did not buy all the required postage stamps at one time, they quickly discovered the obvious reason: the postmistress was a twenty-two year old girl of extraordinary charm and beauty.

Through the postmistress, my sister and I got to know her whole family. Her father, it turned out, was the operator of the light-tower that guarded shipping in that part of the Adriatic. Her older brother was a university student, home on vacation. He was extraordinarily handsome, a fact that did not escape my sister. The postmistress also had several younger sisters whose charm and good looks equalled her own. Their family owned a sailboat, and on moonlight nights my sister and I often went on romantic sailing trips in the Adriatic with the postmistress and her siblings. My knowledge of Italian, which had been rudimentary at the beginning of the summer, was quite fluent at the end of our vacation.

In the years that followed, we went back to Salvore for several more delightful vacations. At the end of the summer of 1930, however, I had to throw myself into serious work, engaging in last-minute preparation for the dreaded comprehensive examination at the end of my university law studies. The written part of the examination took place on November 1930. The grades came out at the end of the year, and it turned out that I was Numero Uno in the State of Bavaria. The oral part of the examination, which took place in January 1931, did not hold any terror; in view of the high grades I had received in the written part, I could not possibly flunk any more.

# CHAPTER VI

# WORK AS A LEGAL APPRENTICE

## Interrupted by the Nazis' Rise to Power

Immediately after passing the examination, I entered upon the second part (the so-called apprenticeship phase) of my legal education. In Germany, as in other civil-law countries, legal education consists of two successive phases. The first one, provided in the form of university study, is essentially theoretical. But this is followed by a second (apprenticeship) phase, which is somewhat shorter and more practice-oriented. During that second phase the candidate, who is now called a Referendar, works as an apprentice or assistant in a civil court, a criminal court, an administrative office, a lawyer's office, and perhaps also in other offices or agencies where legal functions are performed. I went through several of these successive "stations", of apprenticeship training. At the same time I continued to assist my father in his practice.

Under German law, a referendar can be appointed by the court as defense counsel for indigent criminal defendants. One of the clients I thus acquired was a sixteen year old girl who was accused of having committed incest with her father. I got her acquitted by demonstrating that her father had forced her into the illegal act. This acquittal, and a few others that I had brought about, received much publicity in the prison grapevine, with the result that many prisoners petitioned the court to appoint me as their defense counsel. Thus, at the tender age of twenty-one and twenty-two, I suddenly found myself inundated with criminal cases, many of which turned out to be challenging.

At the same time I kept up my interest in commercial law. Professor Mueller-Erzbach suggested that I begin preparation of a doctoral thesis dealing with a topic that focused on the law of unfair competition. Thus, in addition to my duties as a referendar, the work in my father's office and my burgeoning (though unpaid) criminal practice, I threw myself into research on some of the finer points of the law of unfair competition.

I must report, however, that I did not permit my work to interfere too drastically with my social life. My parents were most gracious in opening our house to my friends, regardless of gender. Their particular favorite was a new friend of mine, August Hirschland, a scion of the Hirschland family which I have mentioned before. August, a native of Essen who was a year or two younger than I, spent some time in Munich working as an apprentice for the Aufhauser Bank. He soon turned out to be a most likeable person, highly intelligent and full of fun.

I think he was attracted to our house not only by the warm of my parents hospitality but also by the fact that our week ends and evenings were marked by much fun and laughter – to which August loved to contribute. Father, as I have mentioned, was a great card player, and August frequently joined our bridge games. Those were not serious games; the aim was not to win but to make the other players laugh their heads off, and everybody had an exceedingly good time. On many of those occasions August, with almost paternal pride, showed us photographs of his youngest sister, called Putti, and told us stories highlighting the funny things little Putti had said or done. Judging by the photographs, she was a pretty and somewhat impish redhead. Neither August nor I, however, had any inkling that a decade later Putti and I would fall in love and get married.

August was expected to follow in his ancestors footsteps and to become one of the owners of the Hirschland Bank in Essen. After his apprenticeship period in Munich was over, he was sent to London to continue his study of the banking trade, and subsequently he went to Madrid for the same purpose. In 1934, while in Madrid, he came down with infantile paralysis and was killed by the disease within a few days. A truly tragic end of a life so full of promise and of joie de vivre generously shared with his friends.

Shortly after August left (I believe it was in 1932), his sister Marianne came to Munich as a medical student. She also came to our home quite frequently, thus further, during the semester she spent in Munich Marianne met my cousin Walter Aufhauser, who later became her husband.

In the normal course of events, the period of my apprenticeship training would have ended in early 1934, and I was due to take the second comprehensive law examination in the spring of that year. During 1932, together with three fellow apprentices, I formed a study group in preparation for that dreaded examination. We met once a week and wrestled with difficult questions from former examinations, which were available in the form of a published volume. After a few hours of hard work we often ended our gatherings by emptying a bottle of wine.

Both on the professional and the personal level those years of "apprenticeship" were busy and happy ones, but somewhat overshadowed by an ever-darkening cloud of business depression and political unrest. In the fall of 1930 a national election had taken place from which the Nazis emerged as a very powerful opposition party. In 1932 Hitler challenged Field Marshal Hindenburg for the presidency of the Reich. Hindenburg won, but by then he was a very old man, dependent on his son and other politically unreliable advisors, and the danger of a Nazi takeover became very real.

In Munich, as in other Catholic parts of Germany, Carnival was always celebrated with masked balls and other hilarious festivities. The Carnival celebration which took place in January 1933 was even bigger and more boisterous than its predecessors. Everybody had a vague feeling that the world, as we had known it, was coming to an end, and that this Carnival was our last chance to celebrate. And indeed on the last day of Carnival the Nazis staged the Reichstag fire and took over the German government in Berlin. Old Hindenburg was persuaded, or forced, to appoint Hitler as Chancellor of the Reich, which gave an air of legitimacy and legality to do what in reality was a revolutionary takeover of the central government.

The Bavarian government in Munich held out during the whole month of February and refused to cave in to the central governments demand to nazify all the provincial governments. For a short time Bavaria became a kind of fortress of freedom. Liberal politicians and journalists, and other people who had to fear Nazi persecution, came from Berlin to Munich in order to await further political developments. A small group of Bavarian politicians somewhat amateurishly played with the idea of reviving the Wittelsbach monarchy and of separating the recreated Kingdom of Bavaria from the Nazi Reich. But those dreams did not last long. During the first week of March 1933 the brown-shirted storm troopers took to the streets in Munich and other Bavarian towns, and within a few hours the Nazis took over the Bavarian government. Some of the politicians, journalists and other people known to be opposed to the Nazis succeeded in escaping to Switzerland or Austria at the last minute; but many others were immediately arrested and dark rumors floated about concerning their fate.

The very first to be arrested were those who were suspected of having had anything to do with the plan to re-establish a Bavarian monarchy.

My family and I soon acquired painful knowledge concerning the fate of most of those political arrestees. It so happened that just a few days before the Nazi takeover in Munich my aunt Augusta (called Gusti), the wife of my uncle Martin Aufhauser, was diagnosed as suffering from colon cancer. She underwent an operation, which was so successful that she lived to a ripe old age; but after the operation she had to stay in the hospital for several weeks. While she was there she became friendly with many of the nurses, and every day the nurses told her grim stories of Nazi victims who had been brought to the hospital dying, or already dead, from unspeakable beatings and torture. News got around that near the small town of Dachau, about 20 kilometers from Munich, a concentration camp had been opened by the Nazis. The term "concentration camp" was new at the time, and at first nobody knew what it meant. But soon it became clear that a concentration camp was a sinister place behind barbed wire to which any person suspected of unwelcome political views, and indeed anyone disliked by the new government, could be sent without any legal process, at the whim of the Nazi rulers, and for an unspecified period. As time went on it became known also that most of the guards were sadists and that ferocious beatings and other forms of maltreatment were the order-of the day. Officially, the concentration camps were never mentioned. Anybody who was overheard talking about them was himself in danger of being arrested for slandering the government. At the same time, however, the Nazis did not mind, and indeed secretly fostered, the climate of fear that was engendered by the spreading stories about the camps.

Not surprising for anybody who had familiarized himself with Hitler's books and speeches, the new government immediately began to pursue its anti-Jewish policies. April 1, 1933, was officially declared to be "Boycott Day." The Nazi propaganda machine strongly exhorted all citizens to boycott Jewish establishments on that day. This move, however, had only partial success. A number of people, whether motivated by real anti-Semitism or by fear of the Nazis, did stay away from Jewish-owned stores and other establishments. But many Germans made a point of visiting their Jewish friends and entering Jewish stores and offices on that very day. The Nazis themselves apparently felt that from a propaganda point of view the boycott fell short of a full success; in any event, although their anti-Jewish measures became increasingly oppressive, they never repeated the "Boycott Day."

Propaganda was not the only outlet of the Nazis' anti-Semitism. The main vehicle for implementing anti-Jewish policies was legislation. The aim, as we know today, was the total elimination of "non-Aryans" from German life. This, however, was not accomplished by a single stroke. The Nazis deliberately used what became known as the "Salami Tactics", cutting off one piece at a time. The first decrees eliminating Jews from certain areas of public life made non-Aryans ineligible to hold any position in the media, the film industry, and the theatre. At the same time all non-Aryan judges and other officials were dismissed from public service on the national, state and local level.

The new Bavarian government also issued a decree making non-Aryans ineligible to participate in legal apprenticeship training, and a few days later I received a letter telling me that I was dismissed from such training.

Non-Aryan lawyers' admission to the Bar was revoked; but there were two exceptions, those who had been admitted for more than 25 years, and those who had seen combat duty in World War I, were permitted to remain members of the Bar for the time being. My father, who had been admitted for much more than 25 years, thus was able to continue the practice of law, at least temporarily, and I remained able to assist him.

As I mentioned before, under normal circumstances I would have taken the second law examination in the spring of 1934. Now, in the spring of 1933, it became clear that I would not be admitted to that examination. Thus there was no longer any point in my getting prepared; but some of my colleagues came to me and asked me to help them with their preparation. They offered to pay for that service. I agreed to comply with their wishes, and for a while thus found myself in the position of operating a small cram course.

Having more time on my hands than before, I also decided to intensify the work on my doctoral thesis. I completed the research and notified Professor Mueller-Erzbach that I would deliver the thesis, and submit myself to the oral examination, toward the end of the year. He initially approved that timetable; but in May 1933 I unexpectedly received a phone call from him, asking me to come and see him immediately. When I appeared at his house, he informed me that he had just received rather disturbing news concerning the promotion of doctoral candidates who were Jewish. No such promotion would be possible after the end of the summer semester 1933. He suggested, therefore, that I deliver my thesis within a month and that I take the oral examination in July 1933.

On the part of Professor Mueller-Erzbach it was not only kind but extraordinarily courageous to give me that hint. Under the conditions then prevailing his career would have been endangered if it had become known that he was sharing confidentially obtained information concerning Nazi "Reform" plans with a Jewish candidate. Of course I thanked him profusely for his kindness. At the same time, the conversation threw me into a complete state of shock. The fact was that, although my research was more or less completed, I still had not yet written a single word of the thesis. And there were only three or four weeks left before I had to deliver it!

There was not enough time to write a draft in longhand. Fortunately, my father had a legal secretary who was an excellent stenographer and typist, and who was willing to help me by working overtime. Using the notes I had accumulated during years of research, I dictated the whole thesis (which with its 426 footnotes, came to more than 200 typewritten pages) in two weeks. After another week of making changes and corrections in the first draft, the work was done. As it was clearly a rush job, I was quite concerned that perhaps quality had been sacrificed to speed; but the deadline was upon me, and I had no choice but to deliver the opus to the Faculty of Law. During the weeks that followed, the thesis was read by Professor Mueller-Erzbach, as principal reporter, and by another member of the Faculty as co-reporter. Several decades later, after I had become a law professor in the United States, I had the great pleasure – on the occasion of a trip to Munich – of being shown the reports evaluating my thesis which had been written by Professor Mueller-Erzbach and his co-reporter. Those reports made me blush. At the time, however, the examination process had to go through several additional steps before I was officially told whether I had passed and how my performance had been graded. The next step was a written test of my Roman Law learning. I had to spend a couple of hours all alone in a bare room equipped only with a table and a chair. I was handed a typewritten page containing several paragraphs of a Latin text taken from the writings of a famous Roman jurist (whose name, however, was not mentioned). My task was to (a) translate and (b) explain that text. As I had had hardly any time to refresh my recollection of Roman Law, the whole exercise was quite scary.

But apparently I did not do too badly. The Professor of Roman Law who was in charge of that part of the examination, later told me that my translation was wholly accurate; my explanation, he added with a twinkle, had the virtue of being "novel."

A few weeks later, in July 1933, came the oral examination. During two or three hours I was examined in turn by five members of the Faculty. Many subjects, including Roman Law and Canon Law, were explored in depth, and there was some discussion of points I had made in my thesis. When it was over I was told that the Faculty would now deliberate and that I could learn the result by going to the Faculty office in the late afternoon. White-faced and trembling, I appeared in the Faculty office at the appointed time and was informed that I had passed with the grade summa cum laude. I was told, moreover, that I was only the third candidate in this century upon whom-this rare honor had been bestowed by the Faculty.

Needless to say, a tremendous celebration took place that evening. It was a beautiful summer day. Together with a number of close friends, my parents and I dined in our garden. The celebration lasted well into the night and ended only when the last bottle of champagne had been emptied.

In the months that followed my thesis was published, and in accordance with German custom, I now had to be addressed as "Herr Doktor," which had a very pleasant inflationary effect on my ego.

During the time which I had devoted to my doctoral thesis and the subsequent examination, dramatic changes had taken place all around us. Many of our friends who were "non-Aryan" or "half-Aryan" had lost their livelihood and had to choose between emigration and restructuring their professional lives in compliance with Nazi-imposed restrictions. The choice was always a difficult one, affected by sentimental as well as practical considerations. One does not easily leave a country in which one's family has lived for generations, and whose language and culture one has absorbed since early childhood.

In making these decisions, the affected families also had to consider thorny legal problems. Under a law originating in a decree issued by the pre-Hitler government, any resident of Germany who wished to leave that country had to pay a so-called flight-tax amounting to 25 percent of his or her net assets. Moreover, foreign exchange regulations promulgated by the pre-Hitler government and greatly strengthened by the Nazis made it impossible to take any assets out of Germany without permission of the Foreign Exchange Control Office. Needless to say, to obtain such a permission was exceedingly difficult, expecially for the victims of Nazi discrimination. The net effect of all these laws and regulations was that those who decided to emigrate had to give up most of their earthly belongings and had to start a new life in a foreign country as relative paupers.

Pressure to emigrate – inspite of the material losses suffered by those who left Germany – was particularly heavy in the case of individuals marked by a left-leaning political past. For different reasons, the same special pressure was felt by families with school-age children. In many schools throughout Germany, Jewish children suddenly found themselves ostracized by their former friends and frequently taunted (or worse) by propaganda-infected contemporaries. One way to save children from such suffering was to send them to boarding schools outside of Germany; but many families decided against this solution, either because they found it financially unaffordable or because they did not wish to separate from their children. Thus, for the children's sake, such families were virtually forced to opt in favor of emigration, whatever material sacrifices it might entail.

Among families I knew (regardless of whether they had school-age children) I generally observed that in making the heart-break choice between leaving Germany or staying in the Nazi-infested country the husband often favored staying so long as he was able to earn a living, while women, with greater intuitive foresight, tended to prefer emigration. Many Jewish families were saved from the Holocaust only because the husband wisely decided to yield to the Cassandra-like warnings of his wife.

Families consisting of elderly parents and (married or unmarried) children in their twenties or thirties usually decided that the younger folks should seek a new life in another country, while the parents stayed behind in order to protect their savings from the "flight tax" and the other confiscatory measures by which emigrating people were stripped of most of their property. Decisions of this kind were made by the families of many of my friends. Carl Fulda, who like myself was dismissed from the legal apprenticeship service in the earliest day of the Hitler regime, decided to go to France. His father, a member of the French Legion d'Honneur, had many connections in France; through those connections Carl obtained a work permit and a good job with an insurance company in Paris. His German girlfriend, who was Jewish, joined him in Paris, where they got married and lived happily for a couple of years. In the mid-thirties, however, the French government's attitude toward German refugees became less friendly, and Carl lost his work permit. At that point he and his wife had to migrate again. They came to the United States, where Carl enrolled as a student at the Yale Law School, thus laying the foundation for a more permanent and successful career. His parents had stayed behind in Berlin. His mother was "Aryan," and his father who was Jewish, obviously hoped that his prominence as an internationally acclaimed writer would shield him from the worst excesses of persecution. When that hope turned out to be misplaced, Carl's father committed suicide in the spring of 1939. After his death, his widow succeeded – at the last moment before the outbreak of World War II – in coming to this country, where she joined Carl and his wife.

Ernst Basch, who had been my closest friend in Munich ever since we became classmates at the beginning of our studies at the Wilhelmsgymnasium, also left Germany immediately after the Nazi takeover. He went directly to New York, where under the pen name of E. B. Ashton he authored a very interesting book about Fascism. Later on he became a much sought-after translator of German books into English. His wealthy parents, both Jewish, stayed behind in Munich, where his father died of natural causes; but his mother became a victim of the Holocaust.

It goes without saying that my parents, my sister and I also gave much thought to the question whether we should stay or leave. As our family was exceedingly close-knit, we were reluctant to separate and tended to find a joint solution for the four of us. It took us a long time to reach a final decision. In the light of hindsight, it may seem strange that we remained in Germany for five-and-a-half years after the Nazi takeover; but at the time our reluctance to transplant the family and to sacrifice our savings was not wholly irrational. First of all, there were some good reasons for hoping that the Nazi regime would collapse. The bloody events of June 30, 1934, culminating in the sudden execution, ordered by Hitler, of the head of his Storm Troopers (which was accompanied by mass killings of certain other members and allies of the Nazi party), clearly showed a crack in the unity of the Nazi movement. It was apparent, also, that the Army generals on whose continuing support the Nazi government depended, were by no means unanimous in their admiration for Hitler's person and policies. It so happened that through personal connections we constantly heard fairly reliable tales concerning the attitude of the general staff. There were several periods during which an anti-Hitler coup of the Wehrmacht appeared imminent. We were informed for instance, that in late 1937 and early 1938, when Hitler planned his invasion of Austria (the so-called "Anschluss"), a group of important military leaders headed by General Beck was opposed to that plan and ready to thwart it by overthrowing Hitler. It was only after that group of generals lost its power struggle in the spring of 1938 that Hitler's hold on the government became unassailable, as evidenced by the rapid implementation of his plans for the Austrian "Anschluss." At that point (but only at that point) one had to conclude, and I did conclude, that what was left of the Army leadership would no longer stand in the way of Hitler's aggressive designs and that his acts of aggression would inevitably lead to war.

In order to understand the slowness with which we reached our decision to leave, one has to remember, also that Hitler's oppressive policies against Jewish inhabitants of Germany developed very gradually. It is true that most artistic professions, the media and all public services were "cleansed" of Jews in the early stages of the Nazi regime; but Jewish were initially permitted to remain active as owners, partners or employees of business enterprises. As I have mentioned before, the anti-Jewish boycott attempt of April 1, 1933 was not repeated, and for most Jewish businesses the situation remained fairly stable and tolerable for several years. The Nuremberg Laws enacted in September 1935, which prohibited interracial marriage and sexual relations, marked a distinct hardening of anti-Jewish policies; but even after that, Jewish businesses remained able to function. In 1936 and 1937 many people were under the impression that the situation had stabilized. It was only in 1938, after the "Anschluss" that sharp pressure was exerted to "aryanize" Jewish business concerns.

From 1933 to 1938 my father was still permitted to practice law. My sister, as I have mentioned, had an enjoyable job as pianist-accompanist; and I had the chance of moving into a new and interesting job to be described in the next chapter, which began soon after my doctoral examination and lasted until the upsurge of Nazi terror in November 1938.

# CHAPTER VII

# HOUSE COUNSEL OF A PRIVATE BANK IN NAZI GERMANY

Before, during and after the Nazi period German law has always provided that one does not have to be a member of the Bar in order to become house counsel of a bank, insurance company or other business concern. Of course, a house counsel who is not admitted to the Bar cannot become attorney of record in a litigated case; but under German law he or she may give advice, draft documents and generally handle all non-litigious matters for his or her employer. Such house counsel's inability to handle litigated cases is an element of strength rather than weakness; it enables the house counsel, whenever his or her employer faces litigation, to choose the best outside lawyer as attorney of record (incidentally, this also greatly contributes to house counsel's popularity with other lawyers).

The reader will remember that the Aufhauser Bank in Munich at that time was owned by two of my uncles and a third partner not related to the Aufhauser family. In early 1934, Uncle Siegl conceived the idea that having obtained my doctorate and having had quite a bit of practical experience in legal matters, I should become house counsel of the bank.

The bank, like all banks, had suffered some losses during the depression of the early nineteen-thirties, but had survived and was going uphill again; its legal problems, however, had multiplied as it attempted to salvage credits and collaterals that had gone sour during the depression. My uncles, who had been bankers throughout their adult lives, had no legal training; the person ultimately responsible for the supervision of the bank's legal affairs was the third partner, Emil Kraemer, who was a lawyer. Kraemer and his wife Elisabeth (who was the younger sister of our intimate friend "Aunt Irma") had always been friendly with my parents, and since early childhood I had seen them from time to time. Now all of a sudden Kraemer was my boss, and I did not really know him too well. It was only in the course of my work for him that I came to know him better and to respect and admire him.

Kraemer decided – wisely, I suppose – to try out my legal talent before hiring me as full-time house counsel. Thus, by way of initial part-time employment, he asked me to work on several matters that had proved to be particularly thorny. The most important of these was the so-called Mueller case. The defendant in the action brought by Mueller was an industrial enterprise wholly owned by the bank. The action was for such a large amount that if Mueller had succeeded the defendant might have been bankrupted, with the result that the bank would have suffered a severe and perhaps catastrophic loss.

Just before I was brought into the case in early 1934, the court of first instance, after 15 years of litigation, had entered a judgment in favor of plaintiff Mueller. When I started to study the file of the case, which was seven feet high, I was told to give it my all. And I did.

After several weeks of day-and-night work, I concluded that the court of first instance had overlooked an intricate but clear rule of contract law developed in a long line of decisions of the German Supreme Court. On the basis of that conclusion, I drafted the defendant's brief on appeal. Not being a member of the Bar, I could not sign the brief. It was submitted to the intermediate appellate court by the defendant's attorney of record; but every word in the brief was my language. Kraemer liked the brief, but he was still worried. "A lot rides on this brief," he said to me, and I could not have agreed more, knowing that my job was riding on it.

After an astonishingly short period of deliberation, the intermediate appellate court reversed the judgment of the court of first instance and dismissed Mueller's action. Total victory! There was jubilation among the partners and managers of the bank, and not very long thereafter I was put on the bank's payroll as full-time house counsel.

I shared an office with the other, considerably older house counsel, Dr. Robert Meyer, an excellent lawyer and persistent chain smoker. Our office was so filled with cigarette smoke that one could hardly see the door or window. Whenever Dr. Meyer left the office for an instant, I ripped open all the windows, only to have them closed again by Dr. Meyer, who was a most pleasant and decent human being but philosophically opposed to anything resembling fresh air. He always lectured me that "many people have died from exposure to cold but nobody has ever died from smoky air".

Little did he know that several decades later his statement would be proved totally wrong by scientific research.

Apart from the little controversy over fresh air, however, Dr. Meyer and I got along famously. He was, of course, much more experienced than I, and I learned a great deal from him. As there was more than enough work for both of us, we divided the load in an equitable manner.

I remained in charge of the Mueller case, which was not completely over because Mueller, dissatisfied with the judgment of the intermediate appellate court in Munich, had filed an appeal to the German Supreme Court, which at that time sat in Leipzig. We had to retain an attorney in Leipzig who was admitted to the rather small and exclusive Supreme Court Bar; but again it fell to me to prepare the brief to be filed in opposition to Mueller's appeal. Several times I had to travel to Leipzig in order to confer with the attorney of record. I also attended the oral argument before the five judges of the Supreme Court's Second Civil Panel who heard the appeal. Mueller's attorney, as the appellant, spoke first. He was repeatedly interrupted by the Presiding Justice (a well known jurist and legal author) who exhibited an astounding familiarity with every detail of the facts and arguments. When our lawyer's turn came to respond, he also was bombarded with exceedingly sophisticated questions from the Bench. As he delivered the answers which I whispered into his ear, I could see that the Presiding Justice looked content and satisfied. of course, I could not say anything aloud; but the Presiding Justice and I had made eye contact and smiled at each other, knowing we were the only two people in the room who knew every aspect of the facts and the legal implications of the case. I returned to Munich in a mood of cautious optimism. About a year later the Supreme Court handed down its decision, essentially affirming the judgment of the intermediate appellate court and forever eliminating the cloud of danger for the defendant and the bank that Mr. Mueller had kicked up. In its opinion, the Supreme Court relied on the very line of cases, overlooked by the court of first instance, which I had dug up in my initial research.

Dr. Meyer and I, constituting the Legal Department of the bank, enjoyed considerable independence in dealing with the broad spectrum of legal problems brought to us by other departments, by subsidiaries of the bank and by its customers. Of course, when questions presented themselves that affected vital interests of the bank or involved important policy issues, we would consult with one of the partners, usually with Kraemer. The partners, including Kraemer, also would call on Dr. Meyer or me whenever legal problems arose in their own work. As a result, I found myself conferring with Kraemer several times a week. As he had no children of his own and was a generation older than I, he developed kind paternal feelings towards me. My own attitude toward him became increasingly marked by admiration for the almost unique combination of shrewdness and unfailing rectitude that characterized the workings of his mind. To work for him and with him was exceedingly pleasant. He recognized that I knew more law than he did, while I always realized that his judgment, based on many years of experience and on sound appraisal of human beings, was truly superior. Physically, he was crippled by a disabling condition – possibly arthritic – of both knees. He could get around only with great difficulty, using two canes, and it was only his unusual willpower that kept him working intensely for long hours. In spite of his physical handicap he was invariably cheerful and kind – a wonderful human being who certainly did not deserve the tragic end waiting for him.

The routine matters which Dr. Meyer and I handled independently, covered the whole range of the legal landscape. Litigated cases, for which we retained outside counsel, made up only a small part of our work – especially after the Mueller case was essentially disposed of. An ever-larger portion of our energy had to be devoted to the problems arising from the complex laws, regulations, ordinances and directives dealing with currency control. Those of the bank's customers who were engaged in foreign trade, constantly needed guidance in order to find their way through the maze of those legal pronouncements. Needless to say, the currency-control regulations also strongly affected Jewish customers who contemplated emigration; those regulations were the main obstacle preventing victims of Nazism from taking their property along when they left Germany.

Fairly quickly I became a real expert in the field of currency control laws. Most of the prohibitions imposed by those laws could be lifted in individual cases by a "license". The power to issue such licenses was vested in the Economics Ministry in Berlin, which delegated this power to local Currency Control Offices. On behalf of its customers, the bank everyday routinely filed applications for such licenses with-the Currency Control-Office in Munich. The more complicated license applications often had to be discussed by us in person with the Currency Control Official in charge. Thus, I got to know many of those officials, and to establish reasonably friendly relationships with them. When they ran into a particularly untreatable legal problem caused by ambiguous or contradictory provisions in the foreign currency regulations, they often called me and asked for advice.

This friendly relationship with the officials who had the power to grant licenses made it possible for me quite often to get around the worst consequences of the Currency Control Laws. By exploiting every possible loophole, I made it possible for many of our emigrating customers to transfer some of their property to foreign countries, even though at a loss. As word got around that our bank was experienced and clever in facilitating emigration, more and more Jewish families brought their accounts to us in order to seek our help in liquidating their German property and in attempting to transfer some of the proceeds abroad. As time went on, the currency-control regulations and tax laws aimed at emigration became more and more rigid, and it required more and more ingenuity to circumvent them. Altogether we were able to help several thousand families of Nazi victims to salvage at least a small part of their property when they left Germany. I had my hand in many of those cases, expecially the most complicated ones.

So long as that kind of work was possible, it seemed worthwhile to stay in Germany; but by the middle of 1938 it became apparent that the Nazi regime would increasingly resort to extra-legal acts of terror, and that the victims would less and less be able to liquidate their affairs and to emigrate in an orderly fashion. At that point I decided that our family should leave. In June, 1938, my parents and I spent the Whitsuntide weekend at a lovely country inn in Langenargen on the shore of the Bodensee. During that weekend I persuaded them that the near-certain prospect of war and of anti-Jewish terror left us no choice but to leave Germany and to "return" to the United States. Father was sixty-eight years old at the time, and Mother was almost sixty. The decision to leave their friends, their house, their other property and their accustomed surroundings behind, and-as impoverished newcomers to start a new life in a country which Father had left as an infant and which Mother had never seen, was not an easy one; but both of them were calm and remarkably free of self-pity. "So long as the four of us stay together, we can do anything", father concluded, and thus the decision was made. I was dispatched to Berlin to talk to my sister. She was the only member of the family who cried, as she realized that our return to the United States would mean permanent separation from her Maestro companion. But she agreed.

We now had to turn to the business of obtaining United States passports. I had previously studied the pertinent legal questions and had obtained legal opinions from lawyers in the United States. As Father was born in the United States, his United States citizenship was beyond doubt, provided we could prove his birth in Philadelphia. Nor was there any question concerning my own case. Being the son of a United States citizen who had previously resided in the United States, I clearly qualified as a natural-born citizen. Some questions had to be resolved, however, concerning-the United States citizenship of the female members of the family. Had Mother, who was born a German national, automatically acquired United States citizenship by marrying Father in 1897? And was there any danger that my sister had lost her United States citizenship by being married, however briefly, to a German citizen in 1928? To our great relief, the answer to both questions turned out to be favorable. Until 1922 it was the law of the United States that a wife's citizenship automatically followed her husband's. Thus under that old rule Mother had automatically become a United States citizen through her marriage in 1897. The old law was changed in 1922 by a Congressional enactment, the so-called Cable Act, which provided that henceforth a woman's citizenship should be independent of her husband's, and that, consequently, a woman should neither acquire nor lose United States citizenship by marriage. Thus my sister, whose marriage to a German citizen had occurred after the Cable Act, had not lost her United States citizenship by that marriage. The end result of all these legal consideration was that all four of us were United States citizens.

The real problem was one of proof. Obviously, the basic piece of evidence we needed was Father's birth certificate. During most of his life Father believed that his birth certificate was unavailable and that the fact of his birth in Philadelphia could be proved, if at all, only by much weaker circumstantial evidence. The reason for that belief was the following: around 1890, when Father's sister Francisca was engaged to be married, she (or somebody on her behalf) wrote to the Vital Statistics Office in Philadelphia in order to obtain her birth certificate, which she needed for her marriage. The answer which came back from Philadelphia was to the effect that the birth certificate was unavailable, because all the older vital statistic records had been destroyed in a big fire. In some way or other, my Aunt Francisca managed to get married in spite of the absence of her birth certificate; but from then on everybody in the family believed that Francisca's and Father's birth certificates were simply unavailable.

When Father told me of the Philadelphia fire and its unfortunate consequences, I was initially caught up in the same belief: that his birth certificate had become a victim of the flames. But after legal training and experience had taught me the need for uncompromising thoroughness in factual investigation, I persuaded Father to try again. Without much hope, and only to please me, he then applied to the Vital Statistics Office in Philadelphia. To his utter amazement, by return mail he received a duly authenticated copy of his birth certificate. The explanation was that my

Aunt had been born in 1867 while Father was born in 1869; the big fire had occurred during the two years between his sister's and his own birth. Unbeknownst to Father, his own birth certificate entered into the records shortly after the fire, had always been available, but his erroneous belief in its unavailability had kept him from asking for it.

In the summer of 1938 we took the birth certificate and the other necessary documents to the United States Consulate in Munich, where we had several discussions with officials, including Consul General Hathaway and Consul Roy Bower. The officials agreed that there could be no doubt concerning Father's United States citizenship, but warned that since this appeared to be a case of dual nationality, the processing of application by the State Department might take several months. They advised that Mother should file her passport application together with Father's, but that my sister and I, since our citizenship was derivative of Father's, should file our applications only after the issuance of Father's passport.

My parents filed their passport applications during the latter part of the summer of 1938. As we had been told to expect some administrative delay, we planned to leave Germany in the spring of 1939. Subsequent events, however, forced us to speed up our departure from Germany.

Meanwhile, the Weinberg family in New York, who for generations had been close friends of ours, invited my sister to come to New York and to stay with them for a few weeks or months in order to become acquainted with American life. We persuaded my sister to accept the invitation, thinking that while in New York she might start looking for a job and perhaps retain a lawyer for the sake of speeding up the handling of our parents' passport applications. She booked a passage from Bremen to New York for the end of September 1938. on the very day of her scheduled departure from Bremen, the crisis caused-by Hitler's threat of invading Czechoslovakia reached its climax. On that day, the infamous Munich meeting between Hitler, Mussolini, Chamberlain and Deladier took place, with the result that Munich was totally cut off from the rest of the world for more than 24 hours. We were, of course, greatly concerned about my sister, not knowing whether her ship (a German vessel) would leave Bremen under the war clouds hanging over Europe. All telephone and telegraph communications to and from Munich were interrupted by the Nazis while the negotiations between the four national leaders were going on somewhere in the city. By using Telex (which was new at the time and which the Nazis apparently had neglected to interrupt) we finally got through to my sister and learned that she was all right but that the departure of her ship had been postponed pending the outcome of the crisis. When Chamberlain and Deladier finally gave in and signed the Munich Pact, handing the eastern part of Czechosolvakia over to Hitler, the world was stunned by this bloodless victory of the aggressor. At the same time, everybody living in Europe was-glad that war had once more been averted; and we were particularly relieved that my sister was now able to sail for New York. But I was fairly convinced that war had merely been postponed, and probably for a short time only. It was abundantly clear that our decision to leave Europe had been a wise one; but I began to worry whether we would get out of Nazi Germany before another war crisis or other sinister events would make it impossible to escape.

During the month of October 1938, Nazi pressure to "aryanize" Jewish businesses became more insistent. Kraemer and my uncles began seriously to consider selling or restructuring the bank in response to those pressures. In the course of a conversation I had with Kraemer I told him of our plans to leave. His response was silent but dramatic. He pulled a diamond ring – probably the most valuable piece of jewellery he owned – from his finger and handed it to me. When I hesitated to accept it, he only said "Take it to America. I don't want the Nazis to get it."

Kraemer's fear that the Nazis would soon confiscate even personal belongings of Jewish owners, was not without foundation. During the summer of 1938 all "no Aryans" residing in Germany had been ordered by a Nazi decree to file a detailed list of every item of their real and personal property with the Nazi authorities. The forms that had to be filled out as part of this "inventory of Jewish property" were incredibly detailed. Failure to file those forms by the prescribed deadline, and any omission of reportable property, was declared to be a crime punishable by long terms of imprisonment. It did not require much imagination to realize that the "inventory" was not taken solely for statistical purposes.

After I had told Kraemer of my family's and my intention to leave Germany, the bank began to look for a lawyer who could take over my job. The idea was to hire my successor early enough so that I could train him before my departure.

One applicant for the job had named my former teacher, the famous Professor Wilhelm Kisch, as a reference. I decided that it would be wise to talk to Professor Kisch in person, and called him in order to make an appointment. As his schedule as well as mine happened to be quite crowded for the next few days, he suggested that we have a chat at his home on November 9, which was a Nazi holiday (in commemoration of the storm troopers who had been killed during the failed putsch of November 1923.) The visit I thus paid to Professor Kisch on

November 9, 1938 took a surprising turn. We spent only a minute or two on the qualifications of the above-mentioned applicant, with whom Professor Kisch seemed to be only mildly impressed. But when the Professor heard that as an American citizen I was about to leave Europe and to sail to the New World, he spontaneously exclaimed that he envied me. He bitterly complained that the Nazis had forced him to lend his good name – and indeed his worldwide scholarly reputation – to unworthy, pseudo-scholarly Nazi enterprises and organizations. Professor Kisch had always been known for his wit and his light-hearted temperament. But on that November morning I found him in a mood of despair, foreseeing the worst possible fate for his country. He wished me luck in the new phase of my life that was to begin in the near future. But neither he nor I knew at that moment that my visit with him would turn out to be the very last function I performed as House Counsel of the H. Aufhauser Bank.

# CHAPTER VIII

# FACE TO FACE WITH NAZI TERROR

The afternoon and evening following my chat with Professor Kisch were uneventful; but early the next morning, November 10, the telephone began to ring and kept on ringing. All the callers were women, close friends and relatives of ours, whose husbands had been arrested during the night or early morning. Soon it became apparent that something big and sinister was going on. This was the end of the night which in history has become known as the infamous Crystal Night (Kristallnacht), and the beginning of the first day of openly terroristic persecution of all Jews in Germany. As the history books record, a Jewish youngster from Eastern Europe had assassinated a young German diplomat who worked in the German Embassy in Paris. Ironically, the victim of that assassination was a perfectly decent human being and not a Nazi at all. But the Nazis used this violent act of a fanatical individual as their excuse for unleashing a carefully prepared and organized terror campaign against all Jews in Germany.

Storm troopers were ordered to assemble wearing civilian clothes, leaving their uniforms at home. Masquerading as irate citizens, they devastated and pilfered Jewish stores.

The windows smashed in the process gave the operation its name: "Kristallnacht." All synagogues throughout Germany were put to flames during the night and early morning of November 10. Fire departments were ordered not to interfere; they went into action only in order to save adjoining buildings.

Disturbed by the anxious phone calls we had received in the early morning of November 10, I called Uncle Siegl, assuming that as a British subject and as the Consul General of the Kingdom of Sweden he had escaped the ongoing wave of arrests. He told me that Uncle Martin, the senior partner of the bank, had been arrested in the early morning, and that Kraemer and his wife had committed suicide. He warned me against going to the bank, where Jewish employees apparently were being arrested, and suggested that Father and I should "join him for breakfast" (the meaning obviously being that his home, as the Swedish Consulate General, would be a safer place for us than our own house). As the emerging pattern of the Nazi action clearly was to arrest all Jewish men, but not any women, we decided that Mother should stay at home for the time being; but Father and I drove to Uncle Siegl's apartment.

There we learned more grim details. Uncle Martin had not only been arrested; in spite of his heart condition he was obviously on his way to Dachau, together with hundreds of other Jewish men, young and old. When around 4 a.m. Kraemer got news of Uncle Martin's arrest, Kraemer and his wife, fearing that Kraemer's own arrest was imminent, immediately proceeded to take the poison pills with which they had long been armed. Kraemer's wife lost consciousness fairly quickly; but Kraemer himself, who was a heavy smoker and accustomed to consuming a certain amount of alcohol, apparently was more immune to the effect of the poison. Fearing that the poison might not do its work before the arrival of the Nazi henchmen, the crippled man dragged himself up several flights of stairs and threw himself out of a window.

Uncle Siegl grimly sat in front of the telephone, making innumerable calls to the many politicians and diplomats, inside and outside of Germany, with whom he was on friendly terms, in a desperate attempt to mobilize enough pressure to get his brother out of the concentration camp. I asked him whether I could be of any help; but as there was only one telephone, which he himself was using without interruption, the answer was in the negative. I decided, therefore, to leave Father in Uncle Siegl's relatively safe apartment and to go out in order to have a look around.

A few minutes from my uncle's apartment I came across the smoldering ruins of Munich's Central Synagogue. There were fire trucks and firemen protecting the adjoining buildings; but the synagogue was permitted to burn to the ground. In the nearby shopping district I saw the broken windows of Jewish-owned shops. The shops were deserted; but although quite a bit of merchandise was still lying around, people silently passed by and, so far as I could discover, did not help themselves to the merchandise. The passers-by seemed to make a studied effort not to notice the burning synagogue and the shattered, half-empty stores. Nobody said anything in public, but there was no evidence of any enthusiasm inspired by the Nazi deeds of the previous night.

In the course of my walk it suddenly occurred to me that Father's United States passport might be issued any day now and that in that event I would need passport photographs for the purpose of filing my own passport application. As life was evidently uncertain and I did not know what I would be doing the next few days, I thought that this was an opportune time for getting my passport photographs. I walked into a photo shop, had my picture snapped and was told to come back for the finished photographs in an hour.

During that hour I thought I should make a quick trip to our house, in order to get two things which I had neglected to take along in the morning: first, I wanted to arm myself with some cash. As a precaution against confiscatory Nazi measures, I had for some time accumulated a substantial hoard of cash, for which I had found an exquisite hiding place in a cavity right under the roof of our house. The second item I wanted to get was an overnight kit, containing my toothbrush etc., since I did not know where I would spend the next few nights. I took a taxi, not to our house but to a place a block away. I knew that it was somewhat dangerous to enter our house, since the Nazis were undoubtedly looking for my father and me. I suspected that they would be checking our house every few hours. In order to wait for their next visit, I hid in the bushes across the street from our house. Sure enough, after a few minutes three burly fellows appeared and marched into our house. After a short while they came out again, looking disappointed. When they had disappeared, I assumed that they would not be back for a little time, and rushed into the house. There I found our totally terrified housekeeper. From her I learned that Mother had left in order to pay a visit to her friend, Irma Heilbronner, who was totally devastated by the death, the night before, of her sister and brother-in-law (Elizabeth and Emil Kraemer). Needless to say, I did not spend much time at home. I quickly packed my overnight kit and took some cash from the hiding place. Then I left the house and walked to the next taxi station, fortunately without encountering the three burly fellows who were obviously looking for me. I took a taxi back to the photo shop and picked up my passport photos. After that I walked back to Uncle Siegl's apartment, where Father, Uncle Siegl and I, in a glum mood and burdened by all the grim things we had seen and heard, sat down for a quick lunch. As soon as we had finished our meal, the telephone rang. It was Mother, who upon returning home from her sad visit had received a telephone call from the United States Consulate: Father's passport was ready to be picked up!! Having heard this news – a Godsend in the most literal sense of the word – Father and I rushed to the Consulate, which was only a few minutes away. At the entrance, we ran into a number of English and American newspaper reporters, who were avid for news about the ongoing Nazi action. I told them that Martin Aufhauser, the senior partner of the internationally known Aufhauser Bank, was among the many Jews arrested during the previous night, and that by now he was presumably in Dachau. This bit of news made headlines in London and New York the next morning, and it may have saved my uncle's life. He was released after a few days, because at that time the Nazis were still sensitive to bad publicity in other countries, expecially in England and the United States.

After we entered the Consulate, we were greeted by Consul General Hathaway and Consul Bower, who confirmed the happy news that they had just received a cable from the State Department authorizing the issuance of Father's United States passport, which would also be valid for Mother. With trembling hands and tears in his eyes, Father received the lifesaving document. I then immediately proceeded to fill out the forms that were necessary for my own passport application. Fortunately I had the required passport photos, and the officials at the Consulate, all of whom were exceedingly helpful, promised immediately to cable my application to Washington. We all knew that the next day, November 11, would be a holiday in the United States; but the Consul General thought that in view of the many emergencies created by the ongoing Nazi action the officials in the State Department's passport division would be working during the holiday. As it turned out, he was right, and my application was processed quite speedily. In the meantime, however, it appeared unavoidable that for a few days I would still be without a United States passport. In order to provide a modicum of protection during that interim period, the Consulate gave me an impressively official-looking document acknowledging receipt of my passport application.

When Father and I finally left the Consulate, it was late afternoon. As the Consulate was only half a block from Father's office, we decided to take a look in order to see what had happened to the office. As we entered, we immediately saw that all of the files were gone. As part of their "Crystal Night" action, the Nazis had systematically removed and confiscated the clients' files in all of the offices of Jewish lawyers. Apart from the removal of the files, however, the office seemed intact. The office safe had not been broken into. This was fortunate, because Father kept securities and other valuables in that safe. We took all the securities out of the safe, and then drove to Dr. Veit, the attorney of the United States Consulate whom Father knew quite well. We handed the securities over to Dr. Veit, asking him to deposit them in Father's account (which, as we knew, would require some official permission under Nazi laws). We also told Dr. Veit that we were about to leave Germany, and asked him to take care of our affairs after our departure. By the time we had given Dr. Veit all the necessary instructions and signed various powers of attorney, it was seven or eight o'clock. After we left Dr. Veit's office, I suggested to Father, and he agreed, that it was better for us not to be in the same place during the night. Father drove back to Uncle Siegl's apartment. I walked around for a while, beginning to think about where I would spend the night. After a quick dinner in a restaurant, I went to a public phone booth and called Mother. She reported that in the early evening, three Party representatives had appeared, again asking for Father and me. Mother told them that we were all United States citizens, but they were skeptical and insisted on seeing the passport. They also informed Mother that they would stay in our house and not permit her to leave until Father returned. When Father got to Uncle Siegl's apartment, he called Mother. Upon being told about her situation, he immediately drove home. Arriving at home, he showed his United States passport to the Nazi henchmen who declared that they had to take him to Gestapo headquarters, and that it was for headquarters to decide whether the United States passport was sufficient grounds for his release. Mother further reported to me that Father and the three Nazis had left in our car just a few minutes before I called. I told mother I would immediately get in touch with somebody at the United States Consulate. I then called Consul Bower at his home. Fortunately he was there. After I reported the facts to him he said he would immediately call the Counsel General and suggest to him that he get in touch with Gestapo headquarters, protesting Father's detention. His hope was that the Consul General would be able to lodge his protest before Father's arrival at Gestapo headquarters. He asked me to call him back ten minutes later. When I called Consul Bower again, he reported that luckly he had reached the Consul General at the latter's home, and that the Consul General immediately called Gestapo headquarters, strongly protesting Father's detention. The Consul General had been able to speak to one of the head people in the Gestapo's "Jewish Section" he thought that his protest had made some impression. Consul Bower asked to be informed later that evening whether Father had returned home. He made it clear that we could call him at any time during the night. After I had thanked him, he inquired from where I was telephoning. I told him that I was in a public telephone booth whereupon he wanted to know where I would spend the night. When I responded somewhat vaguely that I might find a friend willing to take me in, he suggested that I come to his apartment and stay there until the issuance of my passport. With a great sigh of relief I accepted the invitation.

A taxi brought me to Consul Bower's apartment. It turned out that, although he was a bachelor, he was not living alone. His household was presided over by an elderly aunt of his. The third member of the household was the aunt's daughter, a lively teenager who was a high school senior. All of them were exceedingly friendly and acted as if it were the most natural everyday occurrence to take a complete stranger into their household.

We did not have much time to spend on amenities. Two minutes after I arrived, the Consul General called and reported that he had again telephoned the Gestapo official in charge; the latter assured the Consul General that Father had spent only a few minutes at Gestapo headquarters and that the officials, after examining his passport, had immediately released him. The Consul General was glad to hear that I was at Consul Bower's house. He asked us to verify whether the story of Father's release was true, and to report back to him. I then immediately called Mother and gave her the good news we had received from the Consul General; but Father had not yet returned home. I asked mother to call me immediately as soon as he returned.

The next ten minutes were full of tension. We thought that the Gestapo official's statement to the Consul General was probably true; but of course we could not be sure.

Luckily, after ten minutes that seemed like a century, the telephone rang. It was Mother who reported that Father had returned home, tired and dejected, but otherwise intact. As telephones were apt to be bugged, Mother gave no further details. Later I heard from Father that his trip to Gestapo headquarters, although brief, was a harrowing one. As he crossed the courtyard and the corridors on his way to the office of one of the high officials, he saw hundreds of Jews, young and old, who in the roughest manner, were being pushed and thrown into trucks, obviously on their way to Dachau. He, on the other hand, was treated politely after he entered the office of the high official. The latter was obviously impressed by the fact that the American Consul General had called him even before Father arrived at Gestapo headquarters. After looking at Father's United States passport, the official curtly informed him that he could go. On his way out, he again saw grim scenes of arrested Jews being thrown into trucks amid curses and threats. When Father reached the street, it occurred to him that the three ruffians with whom he had driven to Gestapo headquarters, had taken his car keys. Father, of course, did not know where the car was. He was in no mood to go back into Gestapo headquarters for the sake of inquiring about the whereabouts of his car. He returned home by taxi (about a year later, our lawyer Dr. Veit obtained payment from the Nazi government for the stolen car, a nice example of the typical Nazi-German pretence of formal legality in the midst of acts of terror and looting).

Consul Bower and I, immediately upon receiving the news of Father's return, called the Consul General, who expressed satisfaction. This also gave me a chance to thank the Consul General for his prompt and effective intervention.

By then it was late. Mrs. Miller (Roy Bower's aunt) showed me into a lovely guest room, and – oh miracle of youth! – I actually slept a good part of the night.

Roy Bower insisted that I not go out so long as I had no passport to protect me. Thus I spent the next few days helping Mrs. Miller with household chores and anxiously reading German and English newspapers. On Monday, November 14th, coming home from the office for lunch, Roy Bower reported that a cable had arrived from the State Department, asking for evidence that I had never served in the German Army. The Consulate had immediately called Uncle Siegl, who within minutes had appeared at the Consulate and had made a sworn statement to the effect that I had never served in the German Army. The contents of that sworn statement having been cabled back to Washington, it seemed likely that the State Department would now grant my application very soon. Indeed, the cable authorizing the issuance of my passport arrived the next day, Tuesday, November 15th. Having said a deeply-felt thank you to my generous hosts, I rushed to the Consulate where I received my passport.

The next thing that Father, mother and I had to do was to make detailed plans for our departure. During the five days I had been in hiding, my parents already had been in touch with the Munich agent of the United States Shipping Company in order to secure passage to New York. It turned out that the next available passage was on the USS Manhattan, which was scheduled to sail from Cherbourg on December 15th. My parents booked passage on that ship for the three of us. The problem was how to pay for the tickets. On November 10th, the day following "Crystal Night," the Nazis had blocked all Jewish bank accounts. Thus, it was impossible to pay by check. In this situation, my above-mentioned hoard of cash came in very handy and made it possible to pay for our trip to New York.

At that point in time – November 15th – the sailing date of our ship was still a month away. It did not seem wise to spend that whole month in Germany. Although up to that point the Nazis had seemed to respect our United States citizenship, one could never be sure how the policy of terror might change over-night.

We decided, therefore, that Father and I would stay in Munich only one more week to take care of the most urgent matters, but that Mother might remain a few days longer to supervise the packing of some of our belongings. We also decided that, until our departure from Munich, Father and I would not sleep in the same place, so that if anything untoward should happen to either of us, the other would remain free to take the necessary counter-measures.

On Tuesday, November 22, 1938 Father and I left Munich by train. Our plan was to travel to Basel, Switzerland, where we hoped to be able to stay with relatives for a few days. Each of us carried a suitcase containing clothes and other personal effects, and each of us had in his wallet the equivalent of $4.00 – the maximum cash amount one was permitted to take out of Germany.

It was a strange but not a tragic feeling to walk away from all one's other possessions – a lovely house, securities, bank accounts, all of which, under Nazi laws, were bound to be "frozen" upon our departure. Even under Nazi laws, one was permitted to have furniture and other tangible personal property shipped to one's new home. We knew, however, that our furniture would be much too large in size for the kind of small apartment in which we would have to live in New York. Thus there was no point in having it shipped to America at great expense. During the few days, she would still remain in Munich, Mother was to select a few paintings, rugs and silverware that could be packed in a couple of cases and shipped to our new home. She actually did so, working day and night during the next four days. What happened to these cases containing our paintings, rugs and silver will be told in a later chapter.

Our trip from Munich to Basel was uneventful. The dreaded Nazi border control turned out to be harmless. The moment the Nazi official saw that we had American passports, he became distinctly friendly, gave us the Nazi salute and left.

When father and I arrived in Basel, we were received most hospitably by my cousin Lilly (a niece of Father's) and her family, consisting of her husband Max and two teenage boys, all of whom had left Germany two years earlier and had started a new life in Switzerland. Before we left Munich, we had arranged with Mother that she would follow us four days later, taking the same train to Basel. Thus on Saturday, November 26th,

Father and I, accompanied by Max, went to the Basel Railroad Station to greet her. The train arrived punctually. Many passengers emerged; but there was no sign of Mother. According to all the arrangements we had made, Mother was supposed to be on that train. We ran up and down the station, but no sign of Mother. The reader can easily imagine the terrifying thoughts that went through our minds. Father and I were so stricken with fear that we did not know any more what we were doing. Fortunately, Max was somewhat more collected. He walked through the train, and in one of the train's compartments he found Mother, fast asleep. Taking care of the things to be shipped to America, giving away many of our other possessions, and saying good-bye to innumerable friends, she had spent several nights without sleep, and when she relaxed on the train, nature finally demanded its toll. When Max brought her out of the train, she fell into our arms, after Father and I had spent what were probably the worst ten minutes of our lives.

We spent a few more days in Basel, and the following two weeks with friends and relatives in Zurich and Strasbourg. Our ship was due to sail from Cherbourg on December 15th. During the last days before our departure from Europe we were in Paris, saying good-bye to a number of friends, including Margaret and Francis Drey, who had come from London to see us off and to discuss what could be done to save Margaret's parents. The latter had attempted to smuggle some property out of Germany and had been caught by the Nazis; they spent some time in jail and were not permitted to leave Germany (two years later they committed suicide).

Even though we were fleeing from our home, leaving virtually all of our belongings behind, our friends seemed to think that we were lucky to be able to escape from Europe. The cloud of Nazi aggression was hanging heavily over Germany's neighbors. In Paris, especially, the mood of the people seemed to be a mixture of fear and cynicism, and under the cover of the eternal glamour of Paris one could sense, also, that Nazi sympathizers were beginning to do their dirty work. To me it became more and more certain that war was inevitable, and when on December 15, 1938, we sailed away from Cherbourg, it felt like being on the last train out of a city to be destroyed.

The Atlantic crossing itself was uneventful, except that the weather – not surprisingly in December – was very rough. Father and I suffered only mildly from seasickness; but poor Mother spent almost the whole week of the trip in bed.

Most of our fellow passengers were German refugees seeking a new home in the United States. Those were the lucky ones, who had applied early enough to obtain U. S. Immigration Visas. Virtually all of the men among them, young and old, had shaven heads, showing that – as a result of the Crystal-Night action or otherwise – they had recently spent some time in a Nazi concentration camp. Father and I were almost the only male passengers with hair on their heads (this was long before I lost my hair, not due to Nazi action, but to ordinary processes of balding).

# CHAPTER IX

# A NEW BEGINNING

On December 22nd we arrived in New York, where my sister, along with several close friends, greeted us at the pier. It was a bitter cold day, and waiting on the pier for our baggage to be unloaded we almost froze to death. But then things began to look up. My parents old friends, Lily and Charles Weinberg, invited us to stay the first few days with them at the Hotel Delmonico and, during the Christmas holidays, at their beautiful estate in Scarsdale.

From my sister I got the wonderful news that a job was possibly waiting for me. At the Dalton School in New York City, a very upper class private girls' school, the regular teacher of German and French had to take a leave of absence because of the imminent birth of a baby, and they were looking for a substitute. Through a friend it had been suggested that my sister should apply for the job; but she had some other plans and thought that I would be better qualified for the job. Thus, a few days after our arrival in the New World, I was interviewed by the Headmistress of the Dalton School. To my surprise and enormous relief, she hired me for the balance of the academic year, my new duties to begin immediately after the end of the Christmas vacation.

My sister meanwhile got a job connected with the 1939 New York world's Fair. In those days, jobs were difficult to come by, and we realized that we were very lucky to be able to support our parents and ourselves without asking our friends for help.

Mother and I found very cheap lodgings at the Willard Hotel on 76th Street between Broadway and West End Avenue (later renamed the Churchill Hotel). In the beginning we had only two rooms for the four of us, which was pretty close living; but that was all we could afford. Later on we were able to rent a second two-room apartment, and from then on our life at the Willard-Churchill Hotel became quite comfortable.

A cross-town bus took me to the Dalton School, which was located at East 89th Street. Returning home from work, I often walked through Central Park, which in those days was still completely safe.

My work, it turned out, consisted mainly of teaching German and German literature; my pupils were girls in the tenth, eleventh and twelfth grades, most of them very attractive and coming from exceedingly wealthy families. When I emerged from the bus in the morning, my pupils arrived in chauffeur-driven limousines.

The Dalton School was probably the world's most progressive secondary school at that time. There were no regular classes. Instead, every instructor posted a detailed assignment, and each student had to decide for herself how much help, if any, she needed from the teacher in order to complete the assignment. Students who wanted help would come to see the teacher in his classroom, which was called a lab. They could come either individually or in groups. To my surprise, the system worked exceedingly well. With the exception of a very small number of problem kids, all the students completed their assignments in time and indeed did very good work. The graduates of the Dalton School usually got into the best colleges and indeed were so well prepared that they could virtually skip most freshman courses in college.

As the students and I got to know each other better, many of them also came to me with their personal problems, most of which had to do with their social life. I still remember a conversation I had with a particularly good-looking senior, who complained about a certain amount of fatigue. The reason for her fatigue was not difficult to guess. It turned out that she went to social events at least five times a week. When I suggested that this was perhaps a bit too much, she looked at me earnestly and said, "Dr. Schlesinger, don't you ever go out?" In the light of the fact that I was then 29 years of age and had a fairly rich social life (not involving Dalton students), that remark struck me as fairly hilarious.

When the academic year ended in June 1939, the Dalton School offered me a permanent job. I felt flattered; but as I had decided to enter law school in the fall, I had to decline the offer. In the meantime, several European friends and former clients, who had managed to bring some money to the United States and who had set up small holding companies for the investment of their money, had asked me to become an officer of those holding companies. The modest salaries I received in that capacity made it possible (just barely) to get by without the pay from Dalton.

During the spring break of the Dalton School I had visited my old friend Carl Fulda and his wife Gaby in Ithaca, where Carl worked for the New York Law Revision Commission. That visit was the occasion for my first look at Myron Taylor Hall, the home of the Cornell Law School, which later on was to become the center of my working life for 27 years.

The week I spent as the guest of Gaby and Carl was most enjoyable, and I was tremendously impressed by the physical beauty of the Cornell campus and of the whole Finger Lakes region. Knowing that there would be an interval of several months between the end of my Dalton job and the beginning of my law studies, I made arrangements for my parents and myself to spend the months of July and August in Ithaca, where life would be more pleasant (and probably cheaper) than in New York City. Thus, the three of us spent the summer in Ithaca, renting – for a trifling amount – a vacationing professor's home on a lovely hillside location.

In the spring, I had applied to the Columbia Law School. This was a relatively easy choice. At that time the law schools of Harvard, Yale and Columbia were the undisputed leaders of the pack. As between the three, there was little difference in quality and prestige, and from my point of view Columbia had the enormous advantage that it was located in New York City, where I could live with my parents, thus avoiding the additional expense of a divided household. The Columbia Law School made my admission dependent on my passing an English language examination. In order to take that exam, I had to travel back from Ithaca for a day. The main part of the exam consisted of innumerable multiple-choice questions. This was the first such examination I had ever taken in my life. When it was over, I was quite depressed. I had not been able during the allotted time to answer all of the questions, and I thought I had surely flunked. As it turned out I had answered more questions than had ever been answered by anyone else, and I passed with flying colors, thus becoming a member of the first year class in September 1939. For my previous law study in Germany I was to be given one semester of residence credit, depending on my academic achievements. Thus, there was a chance that I might finish law school in two and a half years instead of three years.

While we were in Ithaca, the news from Europe that reached us through newspapers and radio (there was as yet no TV) became more and more ominous. At the end of August 1939, Hitler's armies marched into Poland, and World War II began. The immediate effect felt by us was that communication with people in Germany became very difficult. Because of the British blockade of the Atlantic, the only way letters could be sent from the U.S. to Germany was via Japan and Russia. Thus, an exchange of letters took several months. This was a real setback for our efforts, which had gone on ever since our arrival in the United States, to get some of our friends and relatives out of Germany. This took up a major part of our time. To obtain affidavits of support from wealthy American relatives of the people in question, to persuade those relatives or other benefactors to finance transportation and interim stays in Cuba and other places, was truly a major effort. We were successful in some cases, especially that of the Neuburgers, (cousins of Father's and very close friends), who got out of Germany at the last minute and with the help of their American relatives settled down for a happy old age in San Francisco. But we had no such luck in the case of Aunt Irma. The suicide of the Kraemers, her sister and brother-in-law, and our departure had left her in sorrow and loneliness. She was then about 60 years old, and as she was a trained nurse (having served as a nurse for four years during World War I), it seemed likely that if we could get her to New York, she would find a job, especially since she spoke very good English.

We persuaded American relatives of hers to give her an affidavit of support, and wealthy friends of ours were willing to finance transportation and her interim stay in Cuba. Everything seemed to be going in the right direction. The Nazis at that time were in the habit of permitting elderly Jewish women to leave the country. But for reasons we have never been able to clear up, they refused permission in Aunt Irma's case, and she was subsequently deported to one of the Nazi extermination camps, where she became one of the six million victims of the holocaust.

# CHAPTER X

# GOING BACK TO SCHOOL

In September 1939, a few weeks before my thirtieth birthday, I went back to school, as a first year student at the Columbia University Law School. In many ways, the experience turned out to be very different from my student days in Europe. While European law students are simply passive listeners in their lecture courses, American law students are expected to be well-prepared (i.e. to have read and briefed the assigned cases and other materials). My Columbia classmates and I quickly found out that in order to be well-prepared, we had to spend at least two hours, and sometimes three hours, of preparation time for each class hour. And this was by no means a voluntary exercise. In class, the professor would call on individual students to recite the facts of assigned cases and to answer legal as well as factual questions arising in connection with those cases. Woe unto the student who turned out to be unprepared!

Most of the professors, although stern in their demands, were friendly in their exchanges with students. But there were exceptions. Professor Julius Goebel, who taught a legal history course under the title of "Development of Legal Institutions", had a somewhat sadistic streak in him, and to be called upon to recite in his class, was never a pleasant experience. When he called upon one of the few females in our class, he never stopped badgering her until he had her in tears.

The Socratic method used in class discussions quickly revealed the level of my classmates intellectual prowess. I was astounded.

Never before had I been a member of a group of students of such outstanding intelligence. It dawned on me that selective admission can have a pretty powerful effect on the quality of a student body. A large percentage of my classmates had been valedictorians in their college classes, and suddenly I realized that in this highly competitive group I might have to exert myself a little more than I was accustomed to in order to hold my own.

Although most of my classmates were recent graduates and thus were approximately seven to eight years younger than I, I became very friendly with a number of them. What shocked me, however, was that a fairly large percentage of Columbia law students, perhaps as many as one-third, were dedicated Communists. I tried in vain to convince them that any kind of totalitarianism, whether of the Nazi or the Communist stripe, was always oppressive and led to the trampling of human rights. Most of them stuck to their Communist beliefs, and during the days of the Hitler/Stalin Pact were vehemently opposed to any American help to be given to Britain or France. They ran around with huge buttons in their lapels that proclaimed "The Yanks Are Not Coming!" Needless to say, of course, that on June 21, 1941, a few hours after Hitler's surprise attack on Russia, those buttons quickly disappeared.

I was not the only European émigré in our class. There were two others, one of whom, Joseph Kaskell, quickly became a close friend. Joe, who was in his late 40's when he entered Columbia Law School, had been a successful lawyer in Berlin. With his lovely wife, Lilo, and two teenage children, he lived in Queens. He was a grey-haired first year student and doubtless the oldest member of the class. In spite of this age handicap, however, he turned out to be a very good student. For people like Joe Kaskell and myself, who had been steeped in a civil-law approach to legal problems, the necessary adjustment to the common-law way of thinking was not easy. In the legal systems of Continental Europe, which received their decisive intellectual impulses from professors reared in the scholastic method, the starting point in approaching a legal question is always an abstract classificatory idea. The focus of the thoughts that go through the mind of a common-law lawyer tends to be a concrete case, i.e., a particular court's reaction to a particular slice of life. For us European-trained lawyers to get adjusted to this entirely different way of thinking, required a good deal of mental flexibility. For a person of my age this was not too difficult; but in Joe Kaskell's case it was really quite admirable that he was able to summon up this kind of flexibility.

In January 1940, our first examinations came along. I faced them with trepidation. The very first exam was in Civil Procedure, and that turned out to be a rather gruelling experience. The principal question consisted of a complicated fact situation that was wholly predicated on things that had happened to a heifer. The trouble was that, even though by then my English had become pretty good, I had no idea what a heifer was. My first reaction was one of total panic. But then I said to myself: "Rudi, after all you are a lawyer. As a matter of law, a heifer (whatever it may be) can only be either a piece of immoveable property or a piece of moveable (personal) property". The facts showed that the heifer moved around.

Thus it could not be immoveable or real property; and if it was a piece of moveable or personal property, then from a legal point of view it did not make the slightest difference whether it was a piece of jewellery or a kitchen utensil or whatever else I answered the question accordingly, and I got a grade of A.

I did well in all of the courses, and thereby hangs a little tale. As the reader knows, at that time we lived in a West Side hotel, and we always picked up our mail at the desk downstairs, where a friendly young man from Haiti performed the functions of a concierge. At the Columbia Law School, we had to turn in a self-addressed postcard for each course and we would learn of our grades when the law school sent that post card back to us, marked with a grade in the form of a big red letter. Every time one of these postcards arrived, when I emerged from the elevator, the young man from Haiti would shout through the vestibule: "Mr. Schlesinger, you got another A."

During the spring term 1940, one of our courses was taught by Professor Paul Hays, a very fine scholar who later became a member of the U. S. Court of Appeals for the 2nd Circuit. He had been asked by the New York Law Revision Commission to prepare a report on a possible reform of the rules concerning the doctrine of consideration in the law of Contracts. He realized that in civil-law systems the requirement of notarial form sometimes performs a function similar to that of the common-law doctrine of consideration. He was anxious, therefore, to obtain a study comparing the notarial institution in civil-law countries with our own public notaries, and he asked me to prepare such a study during the summer vacation. I was, of course, delighted to accept that assignment, which provided not only closer contact with Professor Hays, but also some much-needed dollars.

I prepared the study for Professor Hays during the first half of the summer of 1940. Very generously, he had it published as an appendix to his own report (See "The Notary and the Formal Contract in Civil Law", 1941 Report of the New York Law Revision Commission, at 403 ff). I had previously published some articles in a Swiss legal periodical; but this was my first publication in English. As it was the first thorough discussion, in the English language, of the civil-law notarial institution, it has received quite a bit of attention and has been frequently cited.

The fee received from the New York Law Revision Commission made it possible for me to devote the second half of the 1940 summer vacation to a trip to California. In connection with the San Francisco World Fair one could purchase a round trip railroad ticket from New York City to

San Francisco for $90.00, and for an additional amount of $10. 00 one could extend the trip to Los Angeles.

After having visited friends in Chicago and Urbana, and after some rubbernecking in Denver, I came to San Francisco, where I stayed at the Cartwright Hotel for $2.00 per night. Coming from the boiling heat of New York City, I thoroughly enjoyed the cool and sunny days I was privileged to spend in San Francisco. visiting old friends in the City and at Stinson Beach, and admiring the beautiful world's Fair exhibits on Treasure Island, I thoroughly enjoyed myself. My only regret was that the days were flying by too fast.

The next stop was Los Angeles, reached by way of a beautiful ride on a train called "The Lark". In the L.A. area I stayed with old Munich friends who lived in an old but – pretty house in Pasadena. In a tiny car, which my friends had acquired for $60.00, we did quite a bit of sightseeing. I intended to visit my cousin, Walter Aufhauser, who had just moved to Los Angeles; but it turned out that he and his family lived very far from Pasadena. As my friends' car did not go faster than 30 miles per hour, we had to figure on a trip of one and a half hours each way in order to visit my cousin. For this reason I kept on postponing the visit. After I had been in L.A. for about a week, my friends suddenly had a chance to borrow a larger and more powerful car for a long weekend, and we decided to use that weekend for a trip to Yosemite and the surrounding parts of the Sierras. The weather was perfect, and the scenery turned out to be exhilaratingly gorgeous. At the end of the weekend, we returned in high spirits to my friends little house, where I was greeted by a bundle of mail forwarded from New York by my parents. One of the forwarded letters was from the Editor-in-Chief of the Columbia Law Review, informing me that 14 members of the first year class (a class of roughly 200) had been elected, on the basis of their grades, to become editors of the Law Review, and that I was one of the 14 lucky ones. The letter also informed me that in order to get an early start on Law Review work, I had to be back at the Columbia Law School three weeks before the opening of the fall term. In order to meet that deadline, I had to return to New York much earlier than planned. In fact, since I had received the letter with some delay, I found myself compelled to leave California almost immediately.

Much of the next day was spent preparing for my return trip. There was only one evening left. Not without a little grumbling, my friends and I decided to use that last evening to make good on the much-postponed visit to my cousin. After a long trip across Los Angeles we found Walter and his wife Marianne (a member of the Hirschland family) in their new home. And with them was their guest, Marianne's younger sister Ruth (called Putti), attractively positioned on the sofa in the Aufhauser's living room. As soon as I saw Putti, I knew I had made the right decision in devoting my last California evening to this visit.

At this point, I must ask the reader to join me in a flashback. As I have mentioned before, friendly relations between the Hirschland and Aufhauser families had existed for a long time. It was natural, therefore, that when August Hirschland, Marianne's and Putti's eldest brother, was being prepared for a future career as a banker, he was sent to Munich for a couple of years to work as a volunteer at the Aufhauser Bank. That was in 1930, and August was approximately 20 years old at the time. He and I became very close friends, and as both of my parents took a great liking to him, he was a frequent guest at our house. We knew from him that he had a little sister who was about 10 years younger than he, and like a proud father he always showed us photographs of that little redhead. August was a person of extraordinary charm and never failing good humor. Among the myriads of amusing stories he used to tell, there were always some that involved exceedingly funny things that his little sister had said or did. Thus, a pretty vivid picture of that little redhead had embedded itself in my mind.

And now 10 years later, to my total surprise, there she set on the sofa, no longer a little brat, but an exceedingly attractive co-ed, and still a redhead. I learned that she was a student at Wheaton College, between her sophomore and junior years, and had just been elected to student government. I told her what I was doing, and for the next couple of hours we conducted a pretty intensive dialogue. Subsequently, I was told by my friends, and Putti was told by her sister and brother-in-law, that during the whole evening neither of us addressed a single word to any other member of the party. When it got late, the dialogue necessarily had to end, but not before addresses and telephone numbers were exchanged. Lighting had struck at first sight.

Early the next morning my friends drove me to the L.A. Railroad Station, and the next several days, with a few stops in between, I was on my way rolling back East. During the train trip I had plenty of time to think about that last evening in Los Angeles. As we were both living in the East, and only vacationing in California, our meeting seemed highly fortuitous. Perhaps fate had something in store. In any event, I began looking forward to our next meeting, after Putti as well as I would return to the East.

Back in New York, I found that my parents, who generally did not know too much about American legal education, had been thoroughly briefed by their friends concerning the value of Law Review service, with the result that they were extremely happy about my entering that service. I immediately reported for duty at the rather dingy offices of the Columbia Law Review in the basement of Kent Hall. Everybody, including even his Lordship the editor in-chief, was very friendly; but there was no mistaking the fact that as a lowly second year student, especially at the beginning of the second year, I was at the bottom of the totem pole constituting the Law Review hierarchy.

Every member of the Law Review staff seemed to take it for granted that to work 16 hours a day, seven days a week, was the very minimum expected of one who wished to belong to the Law Review meritocracy. Writing notes on legal topics way beyond one's horizon, under the stern supervision of a third year student whose horizon did not reach much further, took most of one's time. In addition, there were innumerable other chores, such as citation checking, that tended to keep one up until the early morning hours.

As most of our energy was devoted to the production of the Law Review, not much time was left for class work. In order to keep the grades of Law Review members from slipping, a clever system had been devised called "the purple". Two members of the group were assigned to each course, one to brief the assigned cases, and the other to take class notes. Both the briefs and the notes were then multilithed on a machine using purple ink – hence the name of the system. These multilithed briefs and notes were distributed to all members of the group, with the result that class preparation and class attendance became purely optional, except for the one course in which one was responsible for briefs or notes. Needless to say, the professors did not like the system, but it was so well established that they had to tolerate it. Moreover, those professors whose classes were interesting soon found out that Law Review people usually attended their classes even though it was not strictly necessary in order to get a good grade. Thus my second year in law school was very different from the first, and in many ways more enjoyable.

As the summer vacation ended, Putti came back from California. At that time she lived with her aunt and uncle in Harrison, New York, which is not far from New York City; but as her college was in Massachusetts, there was a chance only for a few dates during the academic year.

In the spring of 1941, to my utter surprise, the third year Board of Law Review elected me to be editor-in-chief for the year 1941–42. This news, together with my photograph, appeared in the New York Times the next day – the only time in my life that my friends and relatives were able to see my picture in the New York Times. I received many congratulations. To my great delight, it turned out that the copy of the New York Times had found its way even to Wheaton College.

I felt at the time, and I still feel today, that there is no other country in the world that offers such opportunities for advancement. Less than two and a half years after I had arrived in New York harbor as a refugee, I had become the editor-in-chief of a leading legal journal, presiding over a staff of 28, and with the power to determine which professors, and other legal authors, articles were to be published.

Needless to say, all these happy events took place against a background of history that was truly ominous. In 1940 Hitler had swallowed Denmark, Norway, Belgium, The Netherlands and France. The British expeditionary force had barely escaped annihilation at Dunkirk. The Nazis' air attack on Britain was in full swing. Western Civilization might have come to a crashing end if Hitler had not, in his orgy of victories, fatefully over-reached himself. That happened on June 21, 1941, when without provocation, and in obvious violation of his solemn pact with Stalin, he sent his armies into Russia. Realizing that this was the turning point of the War, I stayed up all night listening to radio reports, until it became clear that Hitler had really embarked on full scale war against Russia, opening up a second front. The parallel with Napoleon's catastrophic invasion of Russia was, of course, on everybody's mind.

In the early stages of the German-Russian war, however, the string of German victories was overwhelming, and many observers believed that Hitler would do better than Napoleon. Until the Battle of Stalingrad the Russians military position was indeed most precarious. Thus in the spring and summer of 1941 (the period with which we are presently dealing) the hideous specter of a world dominated by Hitler could not be regarded as being totally beyond the realm of possibility.

My own life, meanwhile, proceeded in a happy fashion. During June and July 1941, in addition to never-ending Law Review work, I did research for Professors Jerome Michael and Arthur Nussbaum. Both of them were engaged in exceedingly interesting projects: Professor Michael in Civil Procedure, and Professor Nussbaum in Conflict of Laws. Both of them were true masters in their fields, and I learned a lot, at the same time adding a few badly-needed dollars to my income.

Putti, who by then was between her junior and senior year at Wheaton, during the same period worked as an intern at the Metropolitan Museum of Art in New York City. As the Metropolitan was a lot closer to the Columbia Law School than Wheaton College, this gave us our first chance for really frequent get together. During the week we often had dinner together in the city, and on weekends we would go boating or swimming at the Westchester Country Club (to which she had access through her uncle) or other nice places along the Sound. The flame was growing. In August, we were temporarily separated. Putti again visited her sister in California. I had purchased my first American car – a very old Oldsmobile – in the spring, and during the month of August took a wonderful vacation trip crisscrossing New Hampshire and Maine. Much of that trip was shared with Joe and Lilo Kaskell, who were in the process of looking for a country place in New Hampshire.

Among other adventures, we visited old friends of the Kaskells (a fairly well-known musicologist and his wife), who with their own hands had built themselves a small cottage in a rugged deserted area on the shore of Long Pond, a large freshwater lake on the Island of Mt. Desert. Both Joe and I fell in love with their wonderful, unspoiled part of Maine. A year later, when a 30 acre piece of property on the shore of the same lake was offered for sale, we bought it for $250.00. My share of $125.00 was a large percentage of my total net worth at that time; but I could not resist the temptation of owning a piece of gorgeous wilderness. Long Pond at that time was so clear that one could safely drink from it. There was no road leading to our property. But it was accessible by boat from the other, somewhat more populated side of the lake, and we were told that if we ever wished to build a cottage on our land, we could easily do so by trucking the materials across the frozen lake in the winter and doing the building during the following summer. One encouraging feature of our purchase was that all of the surrounding land – many thousands of acres – was owned by the Rockefeller family. Thus we had nice neighbors. Subsequently, the Rockefellers donated all of their land to the U. S. Government, thereby creating Acadia National Park. When that happened, our property became virtually surrounded by the National Park. The unspoiled nature of the surroundings thus was assured forever.

Upon my return from this New England vacation I sold the Oldsmobile at a loss of $25.00. Law Review work, with the new second year recruits having to be supervised, became even more time-consuming, and sleep began to be a rare and precious commodity.

Putti returned from California – that was the good news. The bad news was that before the month of September was over she had to go back to Wheaton for her senior year. In early October she invited me to come to Wheaton for a weekend. I took the train to Providence, where she picked me up in her lovely grey Pontiac. When we got to the Wheaton campus it seemed that from behind every bush there emerged one of her friends, lying in wait in order to look over Putti beau. These were all lovely – young ladies, and I poured on the charm, knowing that their judgment and advice might be quite important. Apparently I succeeded. Much later I learned from Putti that each of her friends had turned into an eloquent pro-Schlesinger advocate.

During the 1941–42 academic year, there were more weekend meetings, some again at Wheaton and some in Boston, where Putti was permitted to stay at one of two "approved hotels".

One weekend which we did not spend together was the first weekend in December. On the morning of Sunday, December 7th, the terrible news of the "Day of Infamy" came over the radio waves. Normally, I kept away from the Law Review offices on Sundays. But on that particular Sunday, something told me that I should go to the office. I went there around 3:00 p.m., and every one of the editors was there. There was no panic. But the mood was serious. The talk was mainly about whether to enlist in the Navy or in the Air Force. Not too much thought was given to the fate of the Law Review. As it turned out, the demands of military service soon reduced the staff of the Law Review from 28 to 3, the 3 being one woman and two men (including myself) who because of poor eyesight or other physical impairments were rejected by all the services. The three of us put out the remaining issues due to be published during our year. How we did it, I really do not know. But I do remember how it feels to exist on four hours of sleep per night. I do not recommend the experience.

Before Pearl Harbor not knowing of the imminence of war, my Law Review colleagues and I had gone through the usual rounds of job interviews that usually take place during the fall term of the third year. I had received offers from several leading law firms, but delayed a final decision in the hope of obtaining a prestigious judicial clerkship. I had my eye especially on an upcoming vacancy in the New York Court of Appeals, the highest court of the State of New York, where Chief Judge Irving Lehman was said to be looking for a new law clerk. This was a particularly desirable position, not only because of Chief Judge Lehman's great reputation, but also for material reasons. Until the 1930s, these clerkships in the New York Court of Appeals had been treated as political plums, with the result that the salary level (a beginning salary of $4.000.00 a year) was much higher than that offered by any other job available to a recent law school graduate. Chief Judge Lehman had abolished the old practice of filling these jobs through the political spoils system, and had adopted a new custom of hiring top graduates of leading law schools; but the salary level had remained unchanged. Thus this job had the unique aspect of being filled by a merit system but being paid like a political spoils position.

A telephone call from the dean of the Columbia Law School (Dean Young B. Smith) produced an invitation for me to come and have tea with Chief Judge and Mrs. Lehman. The dean admonished me to be on my best behavior, and to be especially careful in handling Mrs. Lehman, who was known to have great influence upon the hiring decisions of the Chief Judge. I went for tea to the Lehmans elegant house on East 71st Street. The Chief Judge immediately impressed me as a man of enormous learning and overwhelming kindness. Mrs. Lehman (whom her friends called Sissy) was a miniscule elderly lady but still very pretty. Her questions were probing, and it was obvious that she was anxious to make sure that the Judge would get the maximum help and support from his clerk. I knew that the Lehmans had been happily married for many years but that they had no children. It was clear that to Mrs. Lehman the Judge was a husband, a child and a grandchild all rolled into one. Because he was hard of hearing, he was a bit handicapped, and Mrs. Lehman obviously watched over him with passionate devotion. I thought that things were going pretty well. It even turned out that I knew some people who belonged to the Lehmans' inner circle. It was quite clear that those people would receive phone calls; but I was pretty certain that they would say nice things about me.

Three days later I received an offer to become the law clerk of the Chief Judge, on the condition that I would stay at least two years – the Judge's theory being that the first year of a law clerk's tenure was needed to break him in, and that he would be really useful to him only during the second year. I gladly accepted that condition. I was expected to graduate from Columbia Law School at the end of January 1942, but I had committed myself to put out the spring issues of the Law Review. For that reason it was agreed that my work for the Chief Judge would begin in March.

Needless to say, during my weekend visits Putti had been kept informed of all the vicissitudes of my job hunt. She was very happy with the outcome.

# CHAPTER XI

# ENTERING INTO MARRIED LIFE AND RE-ENTERING THE PROFESSION

The New York Court of Appeals sits in Albany, but each member of the court has his chambers in his hometown. Thus the Chief Judge had to be in Albany only during the periods when the court was in actual session; otherwise he worked in his chambers in New York City. There were offices for his law clerks both in the courthouse in Albany and in his New York City chambers. At the beginning of March 1942, the Chief Judge handed me my first case, commenting that it was a troublesome case on which the members of the court were in disagreement. I was to prepare a full report on the case; but since I still had to wind up some Law Review chores, the Judge with typical kindness permitted me to do the work at the Columbia Law School Library. Luck would have it that I found a very technical point, until then overlooked by everybody, which disposed of the case. The judge, again with typical generosity, circulated my report among all of the members of the court, informing them that it was the product of his "new law clerk." I could not have wished for a better introduction to the court.

In April 1942, I began to commute to Albany whenever the Court of Appeals was in session. The work was exceedingly interesting. The range of cases reaching the New York Court of Appeals is enormously wide. One day I would work on an upstate farmer's dispute concerning a cow, the next day on the constitutional rights of the Jehovah's Witnesses, and the third day on problems of international law involving the fate of all of the gold of the Banque de France deposited in New York. Criminal cases and domestic relations matters also were constantly on the menu, as were commercial disputes of every description. Very often, I listened to the arguments of counsel, observing the admirable skill and courtesy with which the Chief Judge conducted the proceedings. There was only one thing he could not stand: when a lawyer repeated himself. The mind of the Chief Judge worked so quickly that he always got a point before it was fully stated; but then to have the same point repeated, he regarded as an insult. In spite of his hearing defect, he was able to follow the proceedings quite easily, with the help of a powerful hearing-aid machine built into the desk in front of him. But when a lawyer repeated himself, he would turn off the switch with a loud click which everybody in the courtroom could hear except the Chief Judge. For the lawyers thus cut off that click must have been a rather unhappy experience.

In addition to my work for the court, I had to prepare for the Bar Examination, which took place in June 1942. Of all the many examinations I've taken in my life this was the only one I was really nervous about, fearing that the whole legal profession of the State of New York would roar with laughter if the law clerk of the Chief Judge were to flunk the exam. Fortunately, my fears turned out to be unfounded, and I passed the first time around.

During the first days of July the Court of Appeals held its final session and adjourned until the fall. The Lehmans went on vacation, and there was relatively little work to be done during the summer. That was exactly what Putti and I had been waiting for.

At the end of May Putti had graduated (with honors) from Wheaton. Together with her mother and her aunt I had attended the impressive commencement. Soon after that we began to discuss the wedding date. My proposal, simply to elope, was firmly rejected by Putti, and we fixed September 4th as the great date. On July 11, 1942, we told our respective families, who were delighted and excited, but not terribly surprised. When we told Putti's uncle and aunt with whom she lived in Harrison, her uncle simply said, "the champagne has been on ice for several weeks." We then proceeded to consume it.

The weeks that followed were filled with preparations for the wedding, purchasing of furniture and attempts to find a place to live as a married couple. We decided to live in a suburb rather than in the City, and Putti found a lovely apartment in Larchmont, in a brand new building, where the monthly rent (including a garage) was to be $72.50.

The wedding took place at the Beekman Hotel in New York City. The religious ceremony was performed by the same rabbi who had been Putti teacher when she was a child in Essen. The reception which followed was a very festive affair. As it was a hot and muggy day, consumption of beverages was considerable, and even after Putti and I left, the celebration apparently lasted a long time. Putti's brother managed to attach some bells to the taxi in which we left, and there was quite a commotion as we drove down Park Avenue to the St. Regis Hotel, where we stayed the first night.

When we woke up the next morning, the telephone rang. It was Putti's brother who had decided to try every hotel in New York City; he struck dirt at the third hotel he tried.

Later that day we took a train, which after a good dining car dinner and a night in a sleeping car, took us to Blowing Rock, North Carolina. There, in beautiful surroundings, literally sitting above the clouds, we spent our two-week honeymoon.

Descending from the clouds and returning to the State of New York, we moved into our lovely but as yet only sparsely furnished apartment at Larchmont Acres. Putti, who had studied only intellectual subjects in her college courses, took up cooking with great enthusiasm but little initial experience. To a newly wed husband, however, the food prepared by his beloved always tasted delightful, regardless of its objective condition.

When the court was not in session, I commuted to Chief Judge Lehman's chambers in New York City. Whenever the court was in session, however, I had to be in Albany usually from Monday morning until Thursday or Friday afternoon. During the fall of 1942, and all of 1943, Putti accompanied me on these trips to Albany, where she did volunteer war work for the local Rationing Board and for USO. The Dewitt Clinton Hotel, where we always stayed was only a five minute walk from the courthouse. Thus we were able to have all meals together, and whenever an argument was presented by a particularly famous lawyer or the case itself was particularly interesting, I encouraged Putti to come to the Court of Appeals for her entertainment.

To work for the Chief Judge was enormously rewarding, but also very demanding. No inaccuracy or mistake ever escaped his eagle's work well done. On the other hand he was generous in handing out praise for work well done. His own memory and knowledge of the law never ceased to amaze me. He would say things like this: "I think we had a similar case approximately 11 years ago, which we decided without opinion. Please check whether I am right. " This meant that I had to spend half a night tearing through the court's records of cases decided without opinion; invariably I found that the judge was absolutely right. His ability to forecast the turns and twists in the case law of the U.S. Supreme Court, was equally astonishing. Needless to say, the decisions of the New York Court of Appeals were not normally subject to further review by the U.S. Supreme Court. But in cases involving the U.S. Constitution, a federal statute or some other federal question, such further review is possible. Thus a certain percentage of decisions of the New York Court of Appeals may be reviewed by the U.S. Supreme Court. To my knowledge no

New York Court of Appeals case in which Judge Lehman voted with the majority was ever reversed, and no case in which he dissented was ever affirmed by the U.S. Supreme Court.

While in Albany, the Judge and Mrs. Lehman often invited Putti and me to have dinner at their house (they owned a house in New York City, a house in Albany and a big estate in Westchester County). One evening that stands out in my memory was a seder celebration conducted by the Judge. Among the other guests were some of the non-Jewish members of the Court, who thus were introduced to a fine Jewish tradition, and Charles Breitel, then counsel to Governor Dewey, who much later was himself to become the Chief Judge of the New York Court of Appeals.

I also remember many delightful personal conversations with the Chief Judge. On one occasion, while we were discussing a case before the court that involved a tragic accident in the New York City subway, he said to me with something like real pride: "I know the subway. I have actually been on it." Then, with a smile, he added: "Of course, Mrs. Lehman never has."

The judge's great idols were two men about whom we often talked; Benjamin Cardozo (who had been his predecessor as Chief Judge of the New York Court of Appeals, and then had become a Justice of the U.S. Supreme Court) and Albert Einstein. The latter always spent a few weeks in September at the Lehmans' estate in Westchester. He and the judge became very close friends, and although the judge knew as little of physics as Einstein knew of law, they had many interests in common. Dick Lewis, the judge's stenographer, told us a wonderful story about one of the Westchester visits of Einstein.

September usually is a fairly easy month for the judges of the New York Court of Appeals. The court always opens on the first Monday in October. Thus in September there are no argued cases to decide; the workload consists only of Motions for Leave to Appeal and other motions. Thus the judge normally was able to do all his work in the morning, and Mrs. Lehman was able to organize social events for the afternoon. When Einstein was visiting, this orderly program was occasionally disturbed, because some time during the morning Einstein would walk into the library where the judge was working and the two men would spend the rest of the morning chatting, with the result that the judge had to do his work in the afternoon and that Mrs. Lehman's social plans were disrupted.

After this had happened once or twice, Mrs. Lehman sternly laid down the law to Einstein: "he was not to walk into the library during the morning, while the judge was working there." After a few days, however, the inevitable happened. Einstein, lost in thought on the theory of relativity, had forgotten Mrs. Lehman's edict, and walked into the library. The two men had a delightful chat, and the judge's work had to be done in the afternoon. Mrs. Lehman was fit to be tied. Furiously, she turned on Einstein, with her classical words: "You men are so stupid!"

Of all the cases being decided by the court during the period of my clerkship, the one that received the greatest attention in the media was the case of "Murder, Inc." which involved a group of Brooklyn mobsters engaged in the business of murder for a fee. The enterprise consisted of a very smooth and brainy leader by the name of Lepke (alias Buchalter) and a number of uglies who, at Lepke's direction and under his supervision, actually did the dirty work. In the trial court Lepke and two of his underlings had been convicted of first degree murder and sentenced to death. On their appeal to the Court of Appeals, the defendants' lawyers relied mainly on errors allegedly committed by the trial judge in his rulings on the evidence and in his instructions to the jury. When the case was discussed in conference, it turned out very quickly that the members of the Court of Appeals were divided. The judges' votes were always cast in the inverse order of seniority, with the Chief Judge voting last. When the votes in the Lepke case were recorded, it turned out that the six associate judges were divided 3 to 3. The Chief Judge, whose vote thus was decisive, declared that he was not yet ready to vote and that he needed more time to study the case. For weeks the Chief Judge carried the voluminous record of the Lepke case back and forth between his office and his home. It was clear that to hold the life of those three men in his hands put a severe strain on him, he was not his usual cheerful self, and contrary to his custom in other cases, did not discuss this particular problem with me or with anybody else. I became quite concerned, fearing that the judge might become overstrained or ill. But after a few weeks he appeared in the office early in the morning with a determined look on his face, and called in the stenographer. He dictated for many hours, and when the stenographer began to type, of course I looked over her shoulders and saw that this was the long-expected final opinion in the Lepke case. As the stenographer proceeded to type, I devoured page after page. What I discovered was a long catalog of errors committed by the trial judge and criticized by the Chief Judge. As I read on it seemed clearer and clearer that this was going to be a reversal. But I was wrong. After a twenty page catalog of errors, there followed one final paragraph to the effect that all of those errors were harmless; that the guilt of the defendants was so overwhelming as shown by the record that in spite of those errors the conviction and sentence had to be affirmed. Thus the fate of the 3 mobsters was sealed.

This, however, was not yet the end of the road. Through his Murder, Inc., enterprise Lepke had become a very wealthy man. He hired outstanding lawyers who sought to have the case reviewed by the U.S. Supreme Court, where they argued that at least some of the errors committed by the trial judge amounted to violations of the U.S. Constitution. The argument was ultimately unsuccessful, and the judgment of the U.S. Supreme Court was one of affirmance. The case thus came back to the New York Court of Appeals. In this kind of situation, the Court of Appeals normally would send the case back to the trial court for execution of the latter court's sentence. In the Lepke case, however, it turned out that as a result of the time consumed by the various appeals the date originally set by the trial court for the execution of the defendants had long expired. Thus a new date had to be set, and the question arose whether the new date had to be set by the trial court or the Court of Appeals. I was commissioned to look into that question. I found that similar situations had occurred only very rarely, but that on those rare occasions the resentencing had been done by the Court of Appeals. After looking over whatever authorities I had been able to unearth, the court decided to do the resentencing itself. This, of course, meant that the defendants had to be brought before the Court of Appeals and be given an opportunity for a last statement before being resentenced. The trouble was that the Court of Appeals, where normally only appeals are argued, had no facilities whatsoever to detain dangerous defendants. Rumors began to fly around that the underworld was well aware of the unprotected nature of the Court of Appeals, and that they might make an attempt to get Lepke out of custody on the occasion of his appearance before the court. I was sent to the head of the State Police to discuss the security problems. He told me there was very little the State Police could do. They had only rifles and in case of a serious fight with the underworld would be vastly outgunned. He suggested that we seek help from the FBI.

The FBI promised to take care of any security problem that might arise. All they needed to know was the exact day and hour of the resentencing; we should leave everything else to them. The resentencing was then set for a certain date at 2 p.m., and the FBI was so notified. When I inspected the courtroom a few hours before the time fixed for the resentencing, I saw machine guns placed in every corner. It became very clear that if any attempt were made to spring Lepke and his cohorts, no member of the underworld would survive. Nor would any member of the court or of the audience.

Twenty minutes before two o'clock I walked into the courtroom again. There, on one of the benches reserved for the audience, sat Mrs. Lehman. I respectfully asked her what she was doing here. The answer was: "If Irving dies, I die." A few minutes later, Putti walked into the courtroom. Politely greeting Mrs. Lehman, she sat down beside her. When I asked Putti what brought her here, her answer was a precise replica of Mrs. Lehman's: "When you die, I die." A moment later, a well-dressed lady in her late 30's or early 40 walked in and sat down on the other side of Mrs. Lehman, who obviously did not know the new arrival. I did not know her either, but I strongly suspected (and my suspicion was later confirmed) that the well-dressed lady sitting next to Mrs. Lehman was Mrs. Lepke.

At the stroke of 2 p.m., the Chief Judge opened the hearing. Each of the three defendants was given a chance personally to address the court. Lepke, who looked like a college professor, also spoke like a member of the academic elite. He made an eloquent plea, and so did his lawyer. The other two defendants were unable to express themselves very clearly; but their lawyers, also presented arguments to the court. Of course, as the lawyers probably knew, it was too late for any arguments. The death sentence having been affirmed by the New York Court of Appeals and the U.S. Supreme Court, no open issues were left in the case. What remained to be done was simply to set a new date for the execution of the defendants, and the court promptly proceeded to do that.

There was no attempt to free the defendants, and no shots were fired. The session of the court was adjourned, the defendants were led out by security guards, the newspaper reporters rushed to the nearest telephone, and the spectators began to leave the courtroom. As we walked out together, I told Mrs. Lehman that she had sat right next to Mrs. Lepke, but she was only mildly interested. She seemed surprised and pleased that the affair was over and that no violent incident had occurred. Putti, it seemed, shared those feelings.

During the summer of 1943 Putti and I spent a wonderful summer vacation in Maine and New Hampshire – part of it as guests of Joe and Lilo Kaskell at their newly acquired "house on the hill" in Madison, New Hampshire. It was a happy time, except that for an hour or two every morning poor Putti tended to be quite sick. The explanation of her sickness was that a new member of the family was expected to appear in the Spring of the following year.

In the fall of 1943 Putti bravely continued to commute to Albany with me; but to walk uphill on the steep streets of Albany, especially on State Street, became a more and more strenuous effort on her part. During a social get together Mrs. Lehman asked Putti whether the birth of the expected baby would keep me from accompanying the Judge to Albany. Putti, drawing on the deepest resources of her courage, looked Mrs. Lehman straight in the eye and said "we'll cross that bridge when we come to it." For once, Sissy became speechless. She was not accustomed to anybody standing up to her.

In the meantime, although somewhat delayed by the war, Putti naturalization as an American citizen proceeded in due course. In February 1944, when she was more than seven months pregnant, she was summoned to the New York Supreme Court in White Plains to be sworn in as a new citizen, together with many other successful applicants. When I told Judge Lehman about this, he immediately dictated a letter to the judge who was expected to preside over the swearing-in session. I thanked Judge Lehman for his kindness, but I did not realize what a bombshell effect a letter from the Chief Judge of the State would have upon the judge in White Plains. When Putti and I arrived at the courthouse in White Plains half an hour before the appointed time, we heard a court attendant shouting through the crowds: "Mrs. Schlesinger, Mrs. Schlesinger!" As soon as Putti identified herself to the attendant, she was whisked to the Judge's chambers, and during the whole ceremony she did not sit with the other applicants who were sworn in that day, but sat on the bench right next to the judge. Thus her becoming a U. S. citizen proceeded in real style.

Six weeks later, on March 28, 1944, a native citizen joined the Schlesinger family. This happened, after rather protracted labor at the Fifth Avenue Flower Hospital in New York City. In those days it was usual for the mother and the baby to stay in the hospital for a week. After a week we had to take Steven home to our little apartment in Larchmont. This presented a bit of a problem. It was wartime, and gasoline was rationed. But by saving our rations for several months we had accumulated enough gasoline to be able to drive from New York City to Larchmont.

To give Putti some additional rest, we hired a very kind and experienced elderly lady – Mrs. Schulhofer, a refugee from Nuremberg – to take care of Steven for the first four weeks. Mrs. Schulhofer was essentially of cubic shape; she was as wide as she was high. But she moved with amazing speed and energy and took wonderful care of the baby. When Mrs. Schulhofer left, Putti had to take over. She was very religious about making sure the baby got enough fresh air. But as we lived in an apartment on the sixth floor, she always had to get the baby carriage into the elevator in order to reach the nearby park. For this and other reasons we began to think that it might be preferable to move from the apartment to a house, and we took a good look at those parts of Larchmont which might be desirable and affordable locations.

In spite of Mrs. Lehman's fears, I continued to go to Albany for most of the court's sessions even after Steven was born; but both the Chief Judge and I were aware of the fact that the two years for which I had committed myself to stay as a law clerk had come to an end. I began to look for a new job, which at that point was not difficult at all. I accepted an offer from, Milbank, Tweed and Hope, one of the largest Wall Street firms, and it was agreed that I would start working for them the day after Labor Day 1944. Thus I was able to work for the Chief Judge until the end of the 1943–44 term of the court.

I knew, of course, that a judicial clerkship is meant to last only a limited period of time; but it was with really deep regret that I left the services of the Chief Judge. I knew that I would never again work for or with an individual as kind, as broad-minded, as wise and as learned as Chief Judge Lehman. His literary style may not have been as refined as that of his friend and predecessor Benjamin Cardozo; but in my opinion, if one tries to appraise those two judges as judges, Lehman comes out on top.

At the time I left his service, Judge Lehman was 69 years old. He was to turn 70 in 1945, and under the New York Constitution, as it then stood, had to retire from the Court at the end of 1945. He had interesting plans as to what to do after his retirement, and in the last conversations we had during the spring and summer of 1944, the Judge hinted that those plans might involve further cooperation between him and me. Tragically, a freak accident he suffered in October 1945, a few months before his projected retirement, led to his death due to an embolism, and all those plans came to naught.

During the month of August 1944, my parents had the use of a friend's house in Great Neck, New York, and my Mother suggested that if Putti and I wanted to take a vacation during that period, we could leave little Steven in her care. We accepted the offer, but in order not to put Mother to too much trouble we hired Mrs. Schulhofer to help her during that month. When we left for the railroad station, after having delivered Steven in Great Neck, Putti broke down in tears. She took her first separation from Steven very hard; but she really had no cause to worry. For a whole month Grandmother Schlesinger and Mrs. Schulhofer competed in spoiling Steven, and I do not think that he suffered any hardship. Putti and

I spent the first part of our vacation with Joe and Lilo Kaskell in Madison, New Hampshire, and the second part at the Balsams in Dixville Notch. We received frequent and very positive reports about Steven, and had a glorious vacation.

As soon as we returned, I reported for work at Milbank-Tweed. In accordance with my wishes, I was assigned to the Litigation Department, but at Milbank-Tweed the definition of "litigation" was very broad. On every legal problem which because of its difficulty might lead to litigation, the advice of the Litigation Department was sought. As a result every really interesting question somehow wound up in the hands of the Litigation Department, which nevertheless – in those much less litigious days – consisted of only three partners and four or five associates (much less than 10% of the firm's total manpower).

Among the Milbank firm's clients were the Chase Bank, the Rockefeller family, the New York Stock Exchange and many other important enterprises of finance and industry. My banking background came in handy, but the financial transactions with which I had to deal at Milbank-Tweed were, of course, many times larger than anything I had ever encountered as counsel for H. Aufhauser in Munich. I learned a great deal about high finance, and some of the partners for whom I worked, especially Mr. Timothy taught me some of the finer points of handling witnesses, courts and juries.

During the fall of 1944, Putti and I continued and intensified our search for a house in Larchmont. We finally chose a totally run-down house in a lovely location high on a bluff – 25 Stonyside Drive. The house apparently had been inhabited by incredibly destructive children. Everything breakable was broken, and the house presented itself in such a terrible way that it had been on the market for a long time without finding a buyer. As a result the price had come down to $10,500.00. We concluded that the damage that was visible everywhere throughout the house was essentially superficial, and that the house could be fixed up beautifully at moderate cost. Before making an offer, we obtained the advice of our architect friend Robert Weinberg, who assured us that the house was basically sound and was an ideal fixer-upper.

Under Putti's supervision the fixing-up work proceeded smoothly, even though the carpenter was cross-eyed and quite unable to draw a straight and level line. In January 1945, little Steven, and his parents moved into the new house. When spring came, Steven could play in the yard. On weekends Putti's mother and my parents, and many other friends and relatives came to visit, and in our newly acquired house on the lovely knoll we began to feel like country squires. During the week, of course, I faced a pretty hard commute. While Judge Lehman's office had been within 5 minutes walking distance from Grand Central Station, the Milbank-Tweed office was in the financial district, which meant that after emerging from the suburban train I had to dive into the New York subway.

Every morning, riding the 8:14 commuter train from Larchmont to Grand Central Station, I would devour the New York Times. Those were exciting days for the newspaper reader. The allied armies made steady progress in defeating the Nazis. In the spring of 1945 the war in Europe ended with Germany's unconditional surrender. As the allied armies took hold of Germany and the German occupied territories in Eastern as well as Western Europe, the unspeakable horror of the Holocaust suddenly came to light. In the Pacific, great victories were scored against the Japanese, but in the light of their suicidal tactics it appeared that the conquest of Japan itself would take a long time and be exceedingly costly. Then, one morning in August 1945, with unbelieving eyes, we read about Hiroshima and Nagasaki, I was a little less surprised than most. Although I knew nothing about the Manhattan Project, I had been told by a physicist friend as early as 1940 that there was the theoretical possibility of a new type of bomb thousands of times more powerful than bombs carrying traditional explosives. When five years later I read about Hiroshima and Nagasaki, I remembered that "theoretical possibility."

As the story of the Manhattan Project was made public, Putti remembered that as a teenager she had known Robert Oppenheimer, whose parents were close friends of Putti's uncle and aunt with whom she then lived. – She also remembered that one evening there had been some dispute between her uncle and Robert Oppenheimer about a point concerning Homer's Iliad. The next morning, at breakfast, the dispute was resolved when Robert Oppenheimer quoted the relevant passage in English and in Greek. He had read the entire Iliad – in Greek! – in one night.

I was particularly struck by the story, then revealed for the first time, of Albert Einstein's visit at the White House, in the course in which he persuaded Franklin D. Roosevelt to develop the nuclear bomb before the Germans could. Had Einstein discussed this step, which clearly changed the course of the world' history, with Irving Lehman? I meant to ask the Judge about that, but his untimely death, a few weeks later, made that impossible.

On the domestic side, Putti and I derived much happiness watching Steven as he grew out of babyhood and developed into a real person. Before he was two years old, some of his traits became very noticeable. Except when he was hungry or overtired, he was always friendly, captivating not only his grandmothers but also our other relatives and friends with a charming smile. He was not overly active physically, tending to be a bit lazy, but always keenly observant. He also learned at a very early age how to get his mother's undivided attention, for instance by being excessively deliberate in emptying his bottle.

On weekdays, unfortunately, I saw very little of Steven. The commuter train brought me home so late that Steven was ready to go to sleep, and there was time only for a quick goodnight kiss. But on weekends he and I roamed through Larchmont quite a bit. In the winter, when there was snow on the ground, our old sled was Steven's favorite vehicle, and I derived much pleasure and exercise from pulling the sled through the hilly neighborhood. On one such trip, I ran into a young couple doing exactly the same thing for their little daughter. We struck up a conversation and decided to visit each other. Putti liked the couple (Dotty and Winfried) as much as I did, and a lifelong friendship resulted from that chance meeting.

During most of 1946 Putti's activities were a bit restricted because she was expecting our second child. on December 1, 1946, Steven's monopoly was broken by the birth of his sister June. When we brought her home from Lenox Hill Hospital in New York City, Steven was decidedly unenthusiastic about the new competitor. This unenthusiastic attitude lasted three to four years, but after that they became very good friends.

My work at Milbank-Tweed was consistently interesting and – especially when I worked for Mr. Pfeiffer – very pleasant as well. Much of it was appellate work. The biggest of the cases I became involved in was the famous antitrust case against the U.S. and Canadian aluminum giants – a case that made legal and economic history. We represented the Canadian company, for which (somewhat in contrast to Alcoa, the big American aluminum company) the outcome of the case was essentially favorable. The client, in any event, was very satisfied with the outcome, and thus there was happiness all around.

One other case may be worth mentioning, because it brought me into direct contact with the Rockefeller family. An individual in Buffalo, New York, who was an amateur inventor, claimed that he was the first who had discovered the admixture which, when added to gasoline, enhances its octane power. He, in other words, contended that he was the true inventor of ethyl gasoline. He alleged that representatives of the big oil companies, i.e., of all of the successor companies of Standard Oil, had burglarized his laboratory in the dead of night and in that way had stolen the ethyl secret from him. He demanded damages in the amount of Two Billion Dollars – an amount which probably would have been quite reasonable if his allegations had been true. The plaintiff, who appeared pro se (without a lawyer of record), sued not only all the big oil companies, but also John D. Rockefeller, Jr., as an individual, alleging that the latter had masterminded the evil deed of the oil companies assertedly controlled by him.

Milbank-Tweed represented only one of the defendants, namely Mr. Rockefeller. Each of the defendant oil companies was represented by other law firms, with the result that an army of lawyers handled the case on the defendants' side, while the plaintiff, (although probably advised by some legally trained person, perhaps a disbarred lawyer) officially had no lawyer at all.

Before I got into the case the defendants had repeatedly attacked the plaintiff. Complaint as insufficient in law. Because of the imprecise and loquacious nature of the Complaint, these motions by the defendants were always granted, but invariably with Leave to Amend. The plaintiff always availed himself of the opportunity to amend, and every time he came back with an Amended Complaint, the wording became even more ambiguous and the volume – hundreds of pages – more enormous. Since the plaintiff had no lawyer of record, all of the judges successively dealing with the case were obviously leaning over backwards not to throw the plaintiff out of court. After having studied the case, I pointed out to Mr. Pfeiffer that this game of having complaints dismissed with Leave to Amend could go on forever. My recommendation was to file an Answer, take depositions and force the plaintiff to trial. He agreed with me and persuaded our client as well as the lawyers for the other defendants to adopt this new strategy. I drafted an Answer, which was duly filed. We took the plaintiff's deposition, which – as I had expected – showed that he had virtually no evidence to back up his allegations. The plaintiff then took Mr. Rockefeller's deposition. We successfully moved that that deposition be taken in front of a judge. At the appointed time the plaintiff and Mr. Rockefeller appeared before the judge; Mr. Rockefeller was accompanied by Mr. Evbree, a Milbank partner, and by yours truly. It was obvious from the start that Mr. Rockefeller, who at that time was probably in his 60's, found the experience novel and stimulating, and was having a good time. On the plaintiff's questioning, Mr. Rockefeller patiently explained that he was spending all of his working time on the affairs of the family Foundations, and that he paid no attention to the oil business. He admitted, of course, that he owned large blocks of stock in each of the defendant corporations. When he was asked how he participated in the conduct of those corporations, he explained that every year he received a proxy from each of the corporations; that he always signed the proxy and mailed it back. That was all the plaintiff could get out of Mr. Rockefeller concerning the latter's "domination" of the oil companies. There was no reason for cross-examination. After about half an hour, the deposition was over. Mr. Rockefeller then invited Mr. Embree and me to have a cup of coffee with him at the court's cafeteria. This reduced the Rockefeller fortune by about thirty cents, and we had a very pleasant conversation, in the course of which Mr. Rockefeller told us a lot of interesting details concerning the work of his Foundations. Then he thanked us profusely for our professional help (which had amounted to very little), and the monumental Rockefeller deposition was ended.

A short time later we moved that the case be set down for trial. On the day fixed by the court at 9:30 a.m., the defendants army of lawyers marched into the courtroom, carrying suitcases bulging with documentary evidence. Mr. Pfeiffer appeared for our distinguished client, and I accompanied him, dutifully carrying a bulging briefcase. Everybody looked for the plaintiff, but he was no where to be seen. At 10 a.m., the court attendant called out the plaintiff's name and asked aloud whether anybody was appearing for the plaintiff; but there was no answer. At 10:30 a.m., we sent for the judge, who seated himself on the bench and ordered the attendant again to call the plaintiff's name. Both in the courtroom and in the hall outside of the courtroom, the attendant again shouted whether anybody was appearing for the plaintiff. No response.

When the attendant reported that there was nobody appearing for the plaintiff, the defendants, lawyers moved that the case be dismissed with prejudice. The judge immediately granted the motion, and in this anti-climactic fashion ended the multibillion dollar case. The only thing that remained to be done was to carry all the bulging suitcases back to the respective lawyers, offices, and to send out bills for the successful defense of the case.

There was one other Milbank case which I cannot resist mentioning. In the mid-1940's, some New York City official conceived the idea that the fees received by court reporters for transcripts of court proceedings should be subjected to the City's sales tax. Understandably, the court reporters became very excited about this prospect and decided to fight this tax claim as strenuously as possible. To represent them in this fight, they chose Mr. Pfeiffer – an extraordinary compliment, especially if one considers that these were the most knowledgeable and sophisticated clients. Justifiably,

Mr. Pfeiffer was very proud of this retainer, and I was very pleased when he chose me to assist him in handling this fairly difficult case. We won in all the courts, right up to the New York Court of Appeals. When the latter court's favorable decision came down, I was on vacation, and Mr. Pfeiffer, kind and gentlemanly as ever, sent me a congratulatory telegram.

To his career as a famous trial lawyer no harm was done by the fact that in winning this case he had become the patron saint of the court reporters.

On the home front, the little girl who had arrived on a lovely spring-like day in December ("June in December") brought delight to the hearts of all, with the possible exception of her brother. From the start, June was always a little ahead of what was expected of her. To watch her precocious persona develop, was an unmitigated pleasure. At the same time Putti soon found out that to have to care for two such little ones kept her pretty breathless the whole day and part of the night. For the first few weeks we had a nurse caring for June. She was not nearly as nice as Steven's Mrs. Schulhofer, and we were glad when we got rid of her. But some permanent household help was urgently needed. Our friends Gaby and Frank Marx, who lived not far from us in Scarsdale and whose younger daughter was Steven's age, had a wonderful full time sleep-in maid, a middle aged African American lady. We asked Gaby to talk to her factotum and to inquire of her whether she knew of anybody who could become a housekeeper in the Schlesinger household. As luck would have it, Gaby's maid reported that her own sister, who lived nearby, was looking for a full time job. The sister's name was Frances Thomas. We immediately interviewed her and liked her a lot. She began to work for us, full time, in early 1947, when June was about two months old. During the 28 years of serving as our housekeeper Frances really became a member of the family. For the children she was like a second mother. Whenever the children wanted something and Putti or I said no, they knew how to get it through the back door – from Frances, in whose vocabulary the word "no" did not exist when she dealt with "her" children.

In the summer of 1947 Putti and I, together with Steven and a very nice babysitter, spent a wonderful month in New England, first in Somesville, Maine, near our piece of wilderness on Mt. Desert Island, and then with Lilo and Joe Kaskell in Madison, New Hampshire. While we were away from home, my parents moved into our house in Larchmont, and little June was taken care of by Frances and Grandmother Schlesinger. The latter gave us frequent reports about the daily events indicating that June was going to be a genius. We were told that whenever Grandmother said to June "how tall are you?", June would bring up her hand to point to the top of her head. Not too bad for a seven month old, and in any event enough to make a deep impression on grandparents.

Soon after our return from that glorious vacation, on September 5, 1947, we celebrated my parents golden wedding anniversary. The celebration took place in Great Neck, where my parents for a few weeks stayed in the house of their friends. As part of the celebration, my sister Thea, Putti and I, equipped with wigs and costumes, performed a skit which we had written – a big takeoff on all of the parents foibles. There was much laughter and levity, which turned to surprise insofar as we were concerned. As soon as we were finished with our skit, the parents disappeared and soon returned with wigs and costumes, performing a skit taking off on our foibles. It was a great occasion all around. Underlying the jokes and take off s was the firm knowledge that there was really something to celebrate. Ever since my childhood I had been impressed by the fact that in the midst of all the marital problems bedeviling our friends and relatives, my parents' marriage stood out as a truly loving, fulfilling relationship – a model for those who were to follow.

In the fall of 1947, after having spent three happy and very educational years at Milbank-Tweed, I began to prepare for the next step in my career. I had never been interested in the race to "make partner" in Milbank-Tweed or any other giant law firm. Apart from the fact that in those days it was still exceedingly difficult for a Jewish person to become a partner in any of the big law firms (other than the purely Jewish ones), it had become clear to me that to become a partner was not nearly as attractive as most people thought. At Milbank-Tweed I quickly learned that there were two kinds of partners: the rainmakers and the slaves. As I did not have the connections necessary to become an important rainmaker in a huge law firm, I knew that even as a partner I would be just one of the boys commanded to do the work – at night or on weekends if necessary.

I began talks with some lawyer friends, of my own age or a little older, about setting up our own firm, to which I could have brought some clients, mostly of European origin, who did not fit into a firm such as Milbank-Tweed, but might have brought substantial business to a smaller firm. The talks proceeded to the point where we exchanged drafts of a partnership agreement; but in early 1948 I had to ask my friends to release me from the contemplated partnership, because something new and unexpected had happened.

The new development, which burst into my life almost accidentally and without any previous planning, was the opening up of an opportunity to enter the academic branch of the legal profession. The opportunity arose at the Cornell Law School, which at that time was in the process of building up an International Program. During the years immediately following World War II, law students returning from military service vociferously demanded a greater emphasis on International and Comparative Law. In Europe and Asia, those men had bitterly experienced the wrong kind of international relations. Now they demanded that at least an attempt be made to build international relations on a more solid foundation of international law and of mutual understanding among lawyers across international boundaries.

Of course, Cornell was not the only place where law students returning from the War made such demands. But because of the relatively close relationship between students and faculty that prevailed at Cornell, and because of the farsighted leadership of Dean Robert Stevens, Cornell was just about the first national law school that proceeded to do something in response to the demands of the veterans. The faculty decided that within the confines of existing budgetary limits every attempt should be made to intensify the teaching of International Law and to add Comparative Law to the curriculum.

The International Law part of that decision was consummated with relative ease. Professor Gustavus Robinson, a member of the Cornell Law faculty, although more widely known as a leading expert on Maritime Law, also was an excellent teacher of International Law. But the faculty's decision to add Comparative Law to the curriculum required the hiring of a new faculty member. For budgetary and other reasons, it was decided to look for a candidate who was qualified to teach Comparative Law, but who could also teach bread and butter courses – it being feared that a faculty member teaching only Comparative Law would be regarded by the students as too strange a bird.

After several months of searching, the Cornell Law faculty apparently found it difficult to locate a candidate meeting those requirements. In late December 1947 they discussed the problem with Dean Young B. Smith, the standard-bearer of the Columbia Law School. The reader will recall that Dean Smith was the one who had recommended me to Chief Judge Lehman. In the meantime he had received very positive reports about me from the Chief Judge. Thus he did not hesitate to suggest to the Cornell people that I was just the candidate they were looking for. A few days later, in early January 1948, I received a telephone call from Dean Stevens, who said that he "happened" to be in New York City and invited me to have lunch with him at the Cornell Club. I accepted the invitation with alacrity. At that time I did not know too many places in the United States outside of New York City and its surroundings; but I did know Cornell and the Ithaca area, which both, Putti and I, found very attractive. The lunch with Dean Stevens was a most pleasant affair. Like everybody else, I was tremendously impressed by Dean Stevens, and I hoped desperately that the feeling would be at least in part reciprocal. Indeed, a few days later I received an invitation to come to Ithaca for a one-day look-see visit. Putti, who felt that Ithaca would be a fine place to bring up a family, strongly encouraged me to accept the invitation, and I did so without delay. After a shaky night on the Lehigh valley Railroad I was picked up at 8:00 a.m., at the Ithaca Railroad Station by Dave Curtiss who at that time was the secretary of the Law School faculty. The day turned out to be an uninterrupted round of meetings – with Dean Stevens, with President Day, and with every member of the Law School faculty. It was a gruelling experience. In subtle ways, each faculty member probed into my knowledge, my understanding of the law, my ability to express myself, my background, and all my foibles. By 5:00 p.m., I was truly exhausted, and Dean Stevens kindly suggested that I join him and Mrs. Stevens for "a little drink" and for dinner.

The Dean personally mixed a Martini for me. It tasted very good to me; but nobody told me (what every child in Ithaca knew) that each Martini mixed by Dean Stevens did the work of three. Dinner with the Dean and his charming wife, who knew every Cornell law student by name, was a most pleasant affair. After dinner several key members of the faculty dropped in for more conversation and more drinks. All together I must have had three or four Martinis, a figure which is quite extraordinary if you multiply it by three.

I have no recollection as to what happened thereafter. The only solid facts I know are the following: a) Dave Curtiss told me years later that he got me back to the Lehigh Valley Station in time to make the midnight train back to New York. b) At 7:00 a.m., the next morning I woke up in Perm Station with a splitting headache and with the firm conviction that I had blown it, and that my academic career had come to a sudden and self-inflicted end before it started.

A few days later, however, I was encouraged when by way of a third-hand rumor I heard that Eva Stevens had found me to be "an amusing conversationalist." Several days after that I received an official invitation from Dean Stevens to join the Cornell Law faculty as an Associate Professor at the beginning of the academic year 1948–49; my salary was to be the princely sum of $7,800.00 a year.

Putti and I quickly decided that I should accept the offer. During the spring of 1948 we took several house hunting trips to Ithaca. As all building activity had come to a halt during the War, and the University was growing rapidly, there was a real housing shortage in Ithaca, and the house hunting endeavor at first looked quite hopeless. But one of my new colleagues called our attention to a house on Cayuga Heights Road, which, although it was about to be sold, had not yet come on the market. We quickly snapped it up, and 415 Cayuga Heights Road became our family home for the next 27 years.

Our next worry was that by moving away from the New York City area we might lose the services of Frances. It was with some trepidation that we informed her of our plans; but before we could say anything further, she virtually begged us to take her along to Ithaca. Of course we agreed, but at first we were quite puzzled by her eagerness to move with us. Pretty soon we found out what the reason was. It seems there had been quite a few articles in African American magazines and newspapers extolling Ithaca as a model community where Afro Americans were treated with real respect and had a better life than almost anywhere else in the United States. Frances had read several of those articles, and thus had become quite anxious to move to that model community. She never regretted her decision. Although at the time of our arrival she did not know anybody in Ithaca, she was quickly welcomed into the membership of a very fine Baptist church, where she soon made new friends, and where in time she became one of the leading members of the group. Through her church affiliation she met a very nice middle-aged man, whom she eventually married.

Another problem I had to contend with was of a professional nature. As I mentioned before, I had a number of clients, who would have formed the nucleus of a beginning law practice if I had remained in the New York City area. Most of those clients were of European origin, and their legal problems often had to do with their restitution claims and other property in Europe. In order to remain able to be of some help to those friends and clients even after moving to Ithaca, I suggested to Joe Kaskell that we enter into a partnership, setting up a law office in New York City which in the main would be run by him but to which I would contribute as much time and effort as possible even after moving to Ithaca. He agreed, and we set up the law firm of Kaskell and Schlesinger, with offices at 8 West 40th Street in New York City. It turned out to be a successful enterprise. Working quietly in the Cornell Law Library, I was able sometimes to furnish better ideas and more thorough research than I could have produced in the hub-bub of New York City. My clients became accustomed to dealing with Joe. Occasionally, when especially important questions arose, some of them would come to Ithaca, and periodically I would put in appearances in New York City. Some of the more important matters handled by Kaskell and Schlesinger will be referred to later on.

# CHAPTER XII

# TEACHING LAW AT CORNELL

*[Note to the reader: dictated 8/20/96. Because of Putti's illness, I do not know how much time I can devote from now on to the continuation of this autobiography. Nor can I be certain at this point in time whether I shall ever be able to complete it. But the reader should keep in mind that the part of the story that is yet to be covered will not be irretrievably lost if I should be unable to complete the autobiography. The preceding pages bring us up to the late 1940's. Most of the data set forth on those pages would be unknown to my children and grandchildren and to other interested parties if I had not memorialized them. But as to what happened to the Schlesingers after 1948, other sources are available. The most important family events are stored in the memory of Steven and – beginning in the 1950's – of Fay. And concerning my professional accomplishments during the period of my teaching career quite a number of written sources are available. I should like to call the reader's attention, first and foremost, to the volume entitled "Der Einfluß deutscher Emigranten auf die Rechtsentwicklung in den USA und in Deutschland" by Marcus Lutter, Ernst C. Stiefel and Michael H. Hoeflich, a collection of scholarly papers presented to a large symposium which was held at Bonn, Germany, in September 1991. Two of the papers in that symposium dealt with my work, and one of those (by Professor Friedrich K. Juenger), which begins at page 255 and is entitled "Schlesinger's Influence on the Development of American Law", is in English. Some other articles dealing with my career as a teacher and scholar are cited in Professor Juenger's paper. At pages 490 ff the same volume also contains some reminiscences and comments of my own.*

*Other sources are the article entitled "Rudolf B. Schlesinger: Law Teacher Summa Cum Laude" by Ray Forrester, 17 Hastings International and Comparative Law Review 665 (1994), and the article entitled "Rudolf B. Schlesinger – world Lawyer" by Bertram F. Willcox, 60 Cornell Law Review 919 (1975). Mention should be made, also, of the Summer 1995 issue of The American Journal of Comparative Law (issue in honor of Rudolf B. Schlesinger). Professor Richard M. Buxbaum wrote the Tribute on pages 317–18. Note, however, that in the sixth line of the second paragraph of that Tribute there is a bad misprint. Instead of "understood" it should read "undertook". At pages 477 ff the same issue of The American Journal of Comparative Law also contains my speech accepting the honorary degree conferred on me by the University of Trento, Italy in 1995; and at pages 483 ff there is a bibliography of my writings (which is not wholly complete but will do for practical purposes)].*

Before I actually started teaching, I was under the illusion that teaching law is less strenuous and less demanding than practicing law. But I soon found out that reality is otherwise. A law teacher who seeks success and recognition cannot devote every working hour to the chore of teaching; writing books and articles, acting as a legislative draftsman or as a consultant to government agencies, doing committee work in professional organizations and in one's own law school and university – all of these are necessary parts of the job. In addition, if one wants to stay at the cutting edge of what is actually happening in legal practice at home and abroad, one has to do a certain amount of practical work as counselor or consultant. In spite of all these collateral demands on her or his time, a true teacher will always realize that one's main effort, in terms of interest as well as in terms of time and energy, must be devoted to the task of teaching itself. Every hour of classroom contact requires at least two or three hours of preparation; and quite a bit of additional time is consumed by helping individual students either with their personal problems or in answering the many questions which the classroom discussion has generated in their fertile minds.

Somewhat to my surprise, I found myself working harder than ever before; but I enjoyed every minute of it. I felt like a fish suddenly thrown into water who wonders what has kept him out of the water for so long.

In addition to traditional law courses, in which I was able to use existing case books and other conventional teaching materials, I instituted a new course in Comparative Law. Before leaving the New York City area, I had collected fairly voluminous materials for that course in the dusty basement of the Columbia Law School, where the foreign-law materials were kept. But when the course was offered for the first time in the fall term of 1948, I had not yet gotten around to the task of organizing my collection of materials into assignments for each classroom hour. Dean Stevens helped me by putting an excellent secretary (the wife of a law student) at my disposal. With her help I produced a mimeographed set of cases and other materials for each class hour. Those mimeographed materials were distributed to the students in advance of each class, and by working frantically hard the secretary and I managed to stay approximately two weeks ahead of the students. By the time the term was over in January 1949, I was pretty exhausted; but the exercise had its rewards. I started out with 16 students enrolled in the course; but as time went on, those 16 must have spread the good word among their friends, with the result that toward the end of the course I had almost 100 auditors in addition to the 16 enrolled members of the class.

The 39 installments of mimeographed materials (for 30 class hours) were bound into a pretty massive volume by my secretary. Several copies of that volume were lying on a table in my office. I intended to use them again to teach the same course the next year, but the idea of publishing the materials had not yet occurred to me. In early 1949, while I was in New York City for a few days, a representative of The Foundation Press came to Cornell Law School and asked Professor John W. Mac Donald, with whom he was on friendly terms, whether he thought that any of his colleagues desired to publish teaching materials. John, who was considerably older than I and took a fatherly interest in my career, had the idea of putting The Foundation Press representative in touch with me. He looked for me in my office but found that I was absent. On the table in my office, however, he saw the copies of my mimeographed materials, and on a sudden impulse he gave one of the copies to the representative of The Foundation Press. When I returned to Ithaca, John Mac Donald, who was an extremely busy man, forgot to tell me about the incident. Thus I was totally surprised when a few weeks later I received a letter from the Chairman of Foundation's Editorial Board (Harvard Professor Edmund Morgan), to the effect that they were accepting my comparative law materials for inclusion in the University Casebook Series. Needless to say, I was overjoyed that my manuscript was accepted for publication, even though I had never submitted it.

During the spring, I made some revisions that seemed to be indicated for purposes of publication, and then shipped the manuscript to the West Publishing Company in St. Paul, Minnesota, which did (and still does) the production work for The Foundation Press. In those days the process of printing and proofreading took a relatively long time. The first edition of "Comparative Law, Cases, Text and Materials" saw the light of day in the late spring of 1950. As the first printed course book on comparative law it created quite a stir and was immediately adopted for use in a good number of law schools.

On the personal side, the spring of 1949 was a time of sadness. On March 15th of that year my mother died of a heart attack. We had no warning that anything was seriously wrong with her health. Everybody who ever came into contact with her was truly touched by her gentle goodness. At the same time there was nothing dull about her. She had a wonderful and occasionally mischievous sense of humor and a unique intuitive understanding of other human beings. That she had some kind of a sixth sense, will have become clear to the reader in connection with the ice cave incident which I have narrated above. My sister and I learned early in life that whether small things were involved or important ones, we could never conceal anything from her. Her intelligence and sixth sense always looked through us.

Our father was 79 when this terrible tragedy happened. Right after the funeral we brought him to Ithaca for a few weeks. Watching Steven and June play seemed to get him away from his total sadness at least occasionally. After he returned to New York City, my sister found a lovely elderly lady whom we hired as his companion and who took care of him until he died seven years later.

For Steven and June – and indeed for the whole family, including Frances – Ithaca soon became their true hometown. The children as well as the adult members of the family made new friends and derived much happiness from the scenic and semi-rural surroundings of Cayuga Heights, the Ithaca suburb where our house was located. The distance from our house to the law school was exactly two miles, and as a rule I walked to or from the law school at least once a day.

Under the leadership of Dean Robert Stevens the law school had become a gregarious social center for students as well as faculty. There were numerous enjoyable social events, at many of which Putti, who was in her late 20's and looked even younger, was mistakenly thought to be the wife of a student. As time went on, our circle of friends and acquaintances began to reach beyond the law school, and we became friendly with many faculty members in other departments, including Hans Bethe, the world famous physicist. At a high-brow dinner party we met Vladimir Nabokov, who at that time taught Russian literature at Cornell and turned out to be a very amusing dinner companion.

At the end of 1949 Grandpa Hirschland, who until then had lived in Switzerland, suddenly and somewhat surprisingly arrived in New York City. There followed, during the first three months of 1950, a period of somewhat difficult financial negotiations between him and the rest of the family. Lawyers were bouncing all over the place, and there was a threat of litigation. Fortunately, however, negotiations ultimately led to an amicable settlement, and in the spring of 1950 Grandpa Hirschland visited us in Ithaca and stayed at our house for several days. The children enjoyed his company, and the visit would have been wholly harmonious had it not been for some problems connected with his driving. He was a terrible driver. Indeed, earlier in his life, while he still lived in Germany, he had driven a very powerful automobile straight into a tree, with the result that he suffered a head injury which caused some mental problems during the rest of his life. In Ithaca he committed a number of traffic violations and the police took his car keys away from him. He, however, pulled a second set of keys out of his pocket and drove out of town, presumably in the direction of New York City. Midway between Ithaca and New York City, however, he had another terrible accident, which crippled him for the rest of his life.

During the summer of 1950 we spent a month in a lovely little inn at Long Lake in the Adirondacks. We were accompanied by Judy Kredel, the daughter of a well-known artist. Judy, who was then an undergraduate student at Cornell, had been highly recommended as a babysitter for Steven and June, and she turned out to be a wonderful choice. Steven and June thought that Judy was the greatest thing that had ever come down from heaven, and she became a real friend of the family. The Long Lake vacation was truly perfect. In the middle of that vacation Putti and I had to travel to Scarsdale in order to attend the wedding of my sister and our old friend Lawrence Greig. The celebration took place in the garden of the Weinberg estate; it was a very festive occasion. Although the bride and bridegroom both were in their late 40's, their happy marriage lasted 36 years – until Lolo's death in 1986.

Another event that occurred during the summer of 1950 was the publication of the First Edition of "Comparative Law – Cases, Text and Materials". The book was immediately adopted for teaching purposes in a number of law schools and was widely reviewed in legal periodicals; most of the reviews were very favorable, even though in my own opinion the first edition still had quite a few defects which I tried to remedy in later editions.

The next year (1951) brought my promotion to full professor. In the spring of 1951 it became apparent that in early 1952 Steven and June would be joined by another sibling. This did not prevent us, however, from accepting an invitation to do some summer teaching at the University of Utah in Salt Lake City. By mid-June we had to be in Salt Lake, and since in those days Putti did not believe in flying, we traveled by train.

Steven and June found the trains to be an inexhaustible source of many pleasures, with countless buttons to be pushed and with friendly porters constantly catering to every whim of the children. That June was just coming down with chicken pox was a slight complication; but after two and a half days of rolling West we finally arrived in Salt Lake City. The law school put us up in a sorority house, where we had china and silver for 60 persons and where the children, to their utter delight, were able to spread their toys over 14 bedrooms. The children also discovered, in ways I still do not understand, how to get candy out of the candy machine in the basement without paying for it. Thus, needless to say, Steven and June had a wonderful time. Putti, although visibly pregnant, was still quite mobile at that point, and in conducting the household was helped by Frances, who had arrived by bus a few days after our own arrival in Salt Lake City. At the law school I taught a course on Restitution. The course went very well; the students appreciated my attempt to throw in illustrations taken from Utah cases.

The first few weeks of our stay in Salt Lake City were absolutely lovely, but in July the daytime temperature became very hot. Fortunately, my class was scheduled for early morning, so that on most days we were able to take off around 9 or 10 a.m., and drive up into the mountains where it was tolerably cooler. For several days, however, we had to give up those mountain trips because Steven came down with the chicken pox, and during those days we really suffered from the heat.

Through students and faculty colleagues we learned a great deal about the lifestyle and the beliefs of Mormons, and were much impressed by the manner in which the Mormon community keeps most of their members, and especially their young members, away from crime and drugs and the other less desirable aspects of modern life.

After I finished my course, I managed to grade the examination papers while we were still in Salt Lake. Within a few hours after the grades were posted, a student appeared in my office and told me, purportedly on behalf of a large group of students, that they had thoroughly enjoyed the course and that they wished to express their gratitude in concrete terms. He then produced a present, which by its shape, appeared to be a bottle of champagne. I thanked him profusely and he departed. Five minutes later another student appeared and indicated that he and his friends, being Mormons, had been unable to participate in the present I had previously received. But, he said, they were equally appreciative and also wished to show their gratitude for a fine course in a concrete manner. He then produced another present which by its shape appeared to be a book. After he left, I unwrapped it and found it was the Book of Mormons, which I have kept as a cherished possession ever since.

At the end of our stay in Salt Lake City we picked up the children's toys that were spread over 14 sorority bedrooms, packed our suitcases and traveled West for the rest of the summer. First we stopped at Feather River Inn, a lovely old railroad resort hotel in the high country, where we quickly recovered from the Salt Lake heat. From Feather River Inn we traveled further west to San Francisco, and thereby hangs a humorous tale. The afternoon before our day of departure, I went to the railroad station with eight pieces of baggage that had to be checked. When I arrived there, the station master asked me whether those suitcases were going east or west. My answer was "four east and four west". I have never seen any human being look at me quite the way that station master did. The question which obviously went through his mind was whether to call the police or the insane asylum. The situation improved somewhat when I explained to him that my family and I were on a lengthy trip and that four suitcases, containing our mountain gear and other things we would not need from now on, were to be shipped back east, while the other four suitcases, containing city clothes and other things still needed during the rest of the summer, were going with us to San Francisco and Los Angeles. I do not know whether he completely bought my story; but he did send four suitcases east and four suitcases west (and the right ones at that).

The next day the train brought us to San Francisco, where we stayed at the Clift Hotel and had a wonderful time, meeting old and new friends and showing the sights to Steven and June. Putti, although becoming rounder and rounder, was in very good health and able to enjoy our stay in San Francisco. It was probably at that time that we began seriously to think of San Francisco as a desirable place to which to retire in our old age. More immediately we started looking at the Bay Area as a good place where we might spend our first sabbatical leave.

From San Francisco a very fancy train brought us to Los Angeles where we spent the last week of our vacation with Marianne and Walter. The children, although somewhat younger than their Los Angeles cousins, had a great time, and everybody was sad when the time came to take a train back East.

On January 12, 1952, Fay jumped into this world. The day before June had become quite ill, complaining of a severe pain in her belly. Putti spent the day and evening looking after June; but during the night it became obvious that she had to be rushed to the hospital, which at that time was in the center of Ithaca. We arrived there between five and six in the morning, and at 7:00 a.m., with a minimum of maternal discomfort, Fay was born. After the nurse, who happened to be the wife of one of my students, had given me the happy news, I immediately rushed home to look after June. Frances greeted me with the news that June had a temperature of 105. I thought that Frances had misread the thermometer and checked it myself; but indeed it was 105! I immediately called the pediatrician who, after hearing my report, appeared at our house in no time flat. She was uncertain whether June had appendicitis or some other kind of infection. The problem was very serious. If it was appendicitis, immediate surgery was indicated. On the other hand, if it was not appendicitis, attempted surgery might be extremely dangerous. Fortunately, the leading surgeon of the area was our immediate neighbor. The pediatrician called him over. He came within minutes. I have never seen physicians confer with more serious expressions on their faces. They gave June a penicillin injection and then for the rest of the day came back every hour to check on her. By the end of the day they concluded that it was not appendicitis – a conclusion which fortunately turned out to be correct. My job during the whole day was to keep the truth from Putti, who was feeling fine and was of course happy with the new baby, but at the same time was very suspicious concerning the reports she got about June.

All is well that ends well. By the time I brought Putti and Fay home from the hospital, June had completely recovered. Both Steven and June were wildly excited about the arrival of the new sibling. They never regarded the little one as a competitor and from the beginning had only the most benevolent feelings toward her.

During the spring of 1952 I did a lot of commuting on the Lehigh Valley Railroad. Columbia Law School, my own alma mater, had asked me to teach Comparative Law during that term. At the same time I taught a full load (including Comparative Law) at Cornell. To teach the course at Columbia and at Cornell the same semester, was interesting and quite enjoyable; but it was a strenuous exercise.

So far as Columbia was concerned, their invitation to teach there as a visitor clearly was part of a scheme to lure me away from Cornell; but I discouraged that attempt. With three children happily growing up in Ithaca, it would have been a mistake to move to New York City.

Later in 1952 the Legislature of the State of New York asked the New York Law Revision Commission to examine the most recent draft of the Uniform Commercial Code and to advise the Legislature as to whether (and if so, with what changes) the draft Code should be adopted as the law of New York. It was clear from the outset that the report of the

Law Revision Commission would decide the fate of the UCC not only in New York, but probably throughout the nation. Thus the task entrusted to the Commission was one of signal importance. In order to tackle that task, my friend and colleague John W. Mc Donald, who was the Executive Director of the Commission, assembled an impressive group of experts. I was proud to be chosen as a member of that group. The specific job assigned to me was twofold: the first was to report on Article 5 of the Code, which dealt with letters of credit. Secondly, and more importantly, I was to cooperate with Professor Edwin Patterson of Columbia in appraising the draft Code from a jurisprudential and comparative point of view. It was a great pleasure for me to do this work together with Professor Patterson, who had been one of my favorite teachers when I was a student at Columbia. He and I quickly agreed that he would write the jurisprudential part and I would prepare the comparative part of our report, and that we would compose a joint conclusion. This plan was duly carried out, as the reader can verify by looking at the reports of the New York Law Revision Commission.

The conclusion reached by Professor Patterson and myself was that, subject to necessary improvements in draftsman ship (as suggested by us and by the other consultants) the Code should be adopted in New York.

After the consultants had rendered their reports, the Law Revision Commission held public hearings, in which both proponents and opponents of the Code had an opportunity to express their views. I was invited to participate in some of those public hearings and to help in clarifying the views of those who testified for or against adoption of the Code. The most powerful testimony in favor of adoption came from the Code's chief draftsman, Professor Llewellyn.

The hearings were presided over by Dean Young B. Smith, the Dean of the Columbia Law School. As the reader will recall, Dean Smith had always been exceedingly kind and helpful in supporting my career. But, as was well known among the cognoscenti, his feelings were less kind toward Professor Llewellyn. As a matter of fact, the two men hated each other with a depth of passion that I have hardly ever seen among other people. During the testimony of Professor Llewellyn, Dean Smith presided over the proceedings with an icy courtesy, without attempting to conceal how he despised the witness.

After the hearings ended, it became clear that Professor Mc Donald, the Executive Director of the Commission, and the majority of the Commission's members tended to agree with the conclusion reached by Professor Patterson and myself and thus to favor adoption of the Code in New York. The problem was to persuade Dean Smith to vote in favor of adopting Llewellyn's Code. Professor Mc Donald, who knew that Dean Smith and Professor Patterson were close friends, and that Dean Smith had only the kindest feelings toward me, came up with a scheme that Professor Patterson and I should have dinner with Dean Smith and over a glass or two of the dean's favorite bourbon should try our powers of persuasion. The dinner was arranged, and after dinner the dean asked Professor Patterson and me to join him for "a little bourbon" in his apartment. While the dean kept refilling our glasses (and his own), Professor Patterson and I presented our arguments in favor of adopting the Code. In the early part of the evening, the dean was full of counter-arguments; but as the night wore on and many glasses of bourbon mollified his feelings, the dean's resistance became weaker, and in the early morning hours he agreed to let the Commission vote any way the majority wanted, without registering a dissent which might have kept the Legislature from following the recommendation of the Commission. This is the inside story of how the Uniform Commercial Code became the law of New York and ultimately of the whole nation. It is very clear that bourbon was as essential to the Code's success as legal scholarship.

The subsequent history of the Uniform Commercial Code is, of course, known to those readers who happen to be lawyers. For the benefit of nonlawyers, let me briefly report that, following his after-dinner session with Professor Patterson and myself, Dean Smith convened the New York Law Revision Commission. Without a dissent from Dean Smith, the Commission voted unanimously that, with certain specified improvements, the Code be adopted by the New York Legislature. It was so adopted, and that set the stage for its nationwide adoption. It has been the uniform law of the land for over 30 years, and in the opinion of most observers has been a successful piece of legislation. There can be no doubt that under its aegis the interstate and international trade of this country has enormously flourished.

My own contributions as a consultant have received widespread recognition. Article 5 of the Code was totally redrafted to reflect the suggestions I had made in my report, which therefore has often been cited as an important part of the legislative history of Article 5. More importantly in order to make sure that the Code will always be kept up to date, the American Law Institute International Conference of Uniform State Laws set up a Permanent Editorial Board. That Board has done important work revising and rejuvenating several parts of the Code. It is universally recognized that the idea of such a Board was first suggested in my report on the comparative aspects of the Code. Thus I received quite a bit of credit for the work I had done as a consultant retained by the New York Law Revision commission.

After six years of teaching, members of the Cornell Law School Faculty were entitled to a sabbatical leave. At the option of the faculty member, that leave could be either for a full year at half pay, or for one semester at full pay. Choosing the latter option, Putti and I decided to spend the spring term of 1955 in the West. In preparation for this western jaunt we bought a large station wagon, designed in such a way that little Fay, who was only three years old, could stretch out for a nap after lunch.

Our aim was twofold: to see for ourselves, and to show to the children, a large part of the country; and for a good part of the spring and summer to settle down in Berkeley, where I hoped to do some research at the University of California Law School (Boalt Hall), and where Steven and June would have a chance to go to school.

# ABOUT THE AUTHOR

Rudolf B. Schlesinger has been a towering figure of comparative jurisprudence whose influence has been global. A German refugee scholar, he was educated at Ludwig Maximilian University of Munich and Columbia University and was a professor at Cornell Law School (1948–1975) and University of California, Hastings College of the Law (1975–1996). The "factual approach" he developed in the early 1960s at the Cornell seminars, and the book *Comparative Law*, that reached its 7th edition, have set the methodological standards of the discipline worldwide.

www.ingramcontent.com/pod-product-compliance
Ingram Content Group UK Ltd.
Pitfield, Milton Keynes, MK11 3LW, UK
UKHW021012120926
8556IPUK00039B/1031

9 781839 702761